Journal Keeping

WRITING FOR SPIRITUAL GROWTH

Luann Budd

InterVarsity Press

Downers Grove, Illinois

InterVarsity Press
P.O. Box 1400, Downers Grove, IL 60515-1426
World Wide Web: www.ivpress.com
E-mail: mail@ivpress.com

InterVarsity Press® is the book-publishing division of InterVarsity Christian Fellowship/USA®, a student movement active on campus at hundreds of universities, colleges and schools of nursing in the United States of America, and a member movement of the International Fellowship of Evangelical Students. For information about local and regional activities, write Public Relations Dept., InterVarsity Christian Fellowship/USA, 6400 Schroeder Rd., P.O. Box 7895, Madison, WI 53707-7895, or visit the IVCF website at <www.ivcf.org>.

All Scripture quotations, unless otherwise indicated, are taken from the Holy Bible, New International Version®. NIV®. Copyright ©1973, 1978, 1984 by International Bible Society. Used by permission of Zondervan Publishing House. All rights reserved.

The letter from Abigail Adams to John Adams, March 31, 1776, is reprinted by permission of the publisher from The Adams Papers: Adams Family Correspondence, volume 1, December 1771-May 1776, edited by L. H. Butterfield, Cambridge, Mass.: The Belknap Press of Harvard University Press, copyright ©1963 by the Massachusetts Historical Society.

"A View from the Zoo" is reprinted by permission of the author.

Cover illustration: Boden/Ledingham/Masterfile

ISBN 0-8308-2337-9

Printed in the United States of America ∞

Library of Congress Cataloging-in-Publication Data

Budd, Luann.
    Journal keeping: writing for spiritual growth/Luann Budd.
        p. cm.
    Includes bibliographical references.
    ISBN 0-8308-2337-9 (pbk.)
    1. Spiritual journals—Authorship. 2. Spiritual life—Christianity. I. Title.
BV4509.5 .B83 2002
248.4'6—dc21

                                                                        2001051794

P	19	18	17	16	15	14	13	12	11	10	9	8	7	6	5	4	3	2
Y	18	17	16	15	14	13	12	11	10	09	08	07	06	05	04	03	02	

For Kevin
my one and only

Contents

Acknowledgments | 9

Introduction | 13

Acknowledgments

The ideas in this book have been gleaned over the years from many people who have shared with me how they follow Jesus. I am grateful for the gift of their friendship and how they have shown me the way.

Mom and Dad loved and supported me always (you taught me so much!). Pastor and Mrs. Johnstone laid the foundation. Kent and Myrna McClain led me to experience God's grace. The people at University Fellowship opened their lives and grew me up: Don and Mona Davis, Jan and Bob Spiro, among many others, taught me how to study the Word and walk with the Lord. Gordy first taught me to keep a journal. There is no way to communicate how profoundly your ministries marked me. I learned from watching you.

The faculty at Dallas Seminary and their wives imparted their love for the Word of God and taught me how to study and teach the Scriptures to others: Dr. Howard and Jean Hendricks, Dr.

Stanley and Maxine Toussaint, Mary Seume, Margaret Pentecost. Thank you.

So many dear friends at Redeemer Covenant Church loved us and our children: How can I say thanks for welcoming us into your families and for loving us no matter what? We worked, played and served together: Avis, Ellen, Rose, Sophie, Nikki, Marge, Melinda, Rhonda and Gary, Charlotte, Karleen, Karen, Maureen, Marilyn, Beverley, Lisa and Brad, Joanne and Rick, Bonnie and Steve, Gwenn and Dan. Thank you.

My years spent at the South Basin Writing Project were life-changing: Dr. Ron and Jan Strahl, Dr. Joe and Lisa Potts, Sue, Nancy, Debbie and other teachers who opened the doors to their classrooms and shared their passion for literacy and their insights into teaching. Your commitment to theory and love for teacher research are the foundational pillars of this book.

I am grateful to Janet Graham and Edward Gray for the use of the excerpt from their documentary "The Orphan Trains." I am also grateful to Patricia Emerson Mitchell for permission to use her sonnet "Purpose."

I am also deeply indebted to the women of the Network of Evangelical Women in Ministry (NEWIM). You are my lifeline. You challenge me to keep taking risks and keep pressing hard. You asked me the question that began this book and have encouraged me every step of the way. You read the manuscript and offered wonderful suggestions: Ginger, Susie, Jackie, Marty, Susan, Sunny, Shirley, Sharyn, Christine, Bev, Carolyn, Pam, Sara Jo and all the women who come to The Springs and the Oasis retreats.

This book would not be what it is today were it not for the

support of the men and women at First Covenant, San José. You read the manuscript and gave helpful responses, prayed, took my picture and cheered me on. Whatever I needed, you were there: Maxine, Shirley, Stephanie and Greg, Judy, Christina and Linda. Patty, from the writers conference to the final edits, you walked this journey with me. Thank you.

Ron Lagerstrom, I follow you as you follow Christ. You've introduced me to so many spiritual mentors—the authors you've told me about every month for the last ten years. Your godly wisdom is invaluable. Thank you for leading the way.

I'm so blessed by my children: Jeff and Wendy, David and Sarah, Jason, Shawn and Ashley. I love each of you. You're the best!

Last, I am grateful beyond words to my husband, Kevin, who has treasured me. You are my toughest critic and the one I learn the most from. Week after week your preaching leads me to Jesus. I stand amazed.

Introduction

"What do you do with your journal?"

Although I had kept a journal for twenty-five years, the question stumped me. I had never given it any thought. "I write," was my dumb but honest response.

"Well, then, teach us how."

How do I use my journal? That is the question that began this book. I didn't have a formula or a secret recipe then. I still don't. But through the process of rereading my journals and the published journals of others, I have discovered that I, like most people who keep a journal, use writing to scrutinize all aspects of life and to find God in the midst of the mess.

Last year as I was studying the Bible, I decided it was time for me to come to a conclusion: *What does a vibrant, authentic spiritual life look like?* Over the course of the year I tried to answer this question. I had an image of what it looked like for others, based on biographies and autobiographies. But I wanted to discover what it looked like for me.

One of my conclusions is that to live an authentic spiritual life, I must be a seeker of the Lord. My seeking should lead me deeper in my knowledge of who he is and how I can more intimately love him. My seeking should help me to better understand myself. My seeking should lead me into God's Word to find truth. My seeking should lead me to *see* Jesus and live my life based on his model. Keeping a journal helps me to live as a seeker. As Dallas Willard writes:

> The secret of the easy yoke, then, is to learn from Christ how to live our total lives, how to invest all our time and our energies of mind and body as he did. . . . The secret of the easy yoke is simple, actually. It is the intelligent, informed, unyielding resolve to live as Jesus lived in all aspects of his life, not just in the moment of specific choice or action.[1]

In our journals we can seek to see Jesus and assess our attempts to live like him.

When I was a senior in high school, I lost one of my black diamond earrings. I tore the house apart, retraced my steps, tried to think of every possibility for where it could be. I remember crawling around with my cheek on the floor scanning the carpet at eye level. I felt along the edges of the molding. I spent hours looking. I was intense, unwilling to give up. I had to find it.

I think that's what I'm doing as I write in my journal—I'm seeking, looking for God in the circumstances of my life, in the truths of Scripture, in answers to prayer, in the beauty of nature, in the joy of a child. I am not alone in my search. Jesus has invited me to pursue him, and he leads the way.

My all-out search for my earring left me empty-handed, having apparently wasted a whole day. But a few days later as my mom moved an armchair to vacuum the carpet, there was my earring in the depression left by the foot of the chair.

Throughout Scripture we are promised that if we seek the Lord we will find him. Sometimes our seeking leads us into his presence, where we find his sweetness so profound our words cannot adequately express our adoration. Other times we are left wondering if we wasted our morning. Sometimes we need other people to help us find him. But regardless of our immediate experience, the Lord wants us engaged in the process of seeking. Seeking causes us to grow.

Most of my spiritual seeking takes place in my journal. This book makes visible my search.

This book is for everyone who is willing to explore using writing to grow spiritually. "Part 1: Exploring the Possibilities" discusses what you need to consider as you get started. The first few chapters are for you if you have just purchased your first blank book and want to know how to get it organized. The later chapters of this section focus on foundational principles that will help you to get started writing and stay encouraged. Maybe you have never thought about what you need as a writer. This section surveys what journal keepers down through the centuries have found to be helpful.

If, however, you are already looking for ideas for how to use your journal, you may want to skip part one. "Part 2: Uncovering the Process" answers the question, what do you write about in a journal? First, I write to discover truth through reflection and inquiry. When I use writing to *discover*, I am in the process of thinking about something from various perspectives. I observe what I experience and consider it. I inquire. I turn it over in my hands and ask questions and seek to answer my questions over the course of weeks.

At times I pause in my search for truth and simply *enjoy* the Lord and his creation. I like to draw a cluster of grapes as I'm reading John 15, or create a story for an illustration, or try my hand at writing a poem. Several chapters in this section show various ways to bring creativity into your journal.

Some journal writing is for the purpose of *learning* from secular,

Christian and biblical texts. Certainly discovering insight on my own and learning truth from others are interwoven processes, but for the structure of this book I've made a distinction between thinking new thoughts on my own (discovery) and being instructed by others through reading a book or studying the Scripture (learning) to be instructed by others. So there are some chapters that will help you discover how to be a good reader and how to use writing to help you learn.

"Part 3: Venturing Out" discusses how you can write for a more public audience and how to break through the times when you can't write. I write letters in my journal. I gather illustrations. I write and rewrite. My journal is a resource of ideas I draw upon as I prepare to share with others. But there are times when we can't write, or at least we don't feel like writing. We may not feel very spiritually responsive. Thus I offer chapters on spiritual ups and downs, with encouragement to press on. The book concludes with many ideas you can try in your journal.

Each section can stand on its own. Feel free to skip around.

My desire is that those who believe they cannot write, or who are afraid to even try, will learn to enjoy journal keeping and find it a valuable tool. And I hope that those who have been keeping a journal for years will be energized to pursue new ways of using writing for their spiritual growth. The ultimate goal of journal keeping is not to have ten blank books full of writing. The goal is to experience how deeply we are loved by Jesus and to grow more deeply in love with him.

May Jesus use our writing to transform us into men and women who are lovers and seekers. I hope that we will be amazed by God's grace—and challenged to live holy lives out of deep gratitude for all he has done for us.

Part 1

Exploring the Possibilities

We would see Jesus.

John 12:21 KJV

WHY?
An Invitation to Write

Rise up, my love, my fair one, and come away.
SONG OF SONGS 2:10 KJV

W e are the ones given the responsibility to craft our souls. Twenty-five years ago I was introduced to journal keeping. Just like thousands of Christians before me, I find my private writing is at the core of my search for deeper intimacy with God and my ability to nurture a progressing faith. I use writing to, in Anna Quindlen's words, craft my soul.

> You walk out of here this afternoon with only one thing that no one else has. There will be hundreds of people out there with your same degree; there will be thousands of people doing what you want to do for a living. But you will be the only person alive who has sole custody of your life. Your particular life. Your entire life. Not just your life at a desk, or your life on a bus, or in a car, or

at the computer. Not just the life of your mind, but the life of your heart. Not just your bank account, but your soul. . . . It's so much easier to write a résumé than to craft a spirit. But a résumé is a cold comfort on a winter night, or when you're sad, or broke, or lonely, or when you've gotten back the test results and they're not so good.[1]

Increasingly evangelical Christians are paying attention to matters of the soul. We are learning about spiritual disciplines. We've opened ourselves to the ancient practices of meditation, contemplation and *lectio divina*[2] and are learning how to incorporate periods of silence and solitude into our quiet times. We seek more than an academic understanding of Scripture. We want to love God passionately with all our mind *and* all of our heart and soul. And we want our love to be growing deeper and more passionate as we grow older. We don't want to look back with wistful longing on the passion we had for Christ when we first came to faith.[3] Instead we want to be progressing, growing deeper. The spiritual disciplines are helping us with these matters of the soul. Writing will benefit us too.

Why We Write

The benefits of private writing are numerous. We discover things about ourselves that we never knew. In a journal we can challenge our own thinking and grow beyond the borders of personal prejudices. We can use writing to prepare for meetings, to make the most of evangelistic opportunities, to sort through the pros and cons of issues. Through writing we can also come to understand someone else's perspective, so it helps us resolve interpersonal conflicts. As we write, we can explore our fears and discern our shortcomings.

Writing about our lives is an opportunity to examine our direction, or lack of it, so we can make adjustments. Writing helps us to gain perspective on how we are using time. It helps us to see what is happening around us. In our journals we tell our stories. Private ✓ writing can also be an incubator for public writing and speaking.

We benefit from writing about what we are reading, whether it is something in the Bible or in another book. Writing helps us to analyze, to make connections and to apply truth in our lives. Even copying a passage from the Word of God can help us to experience the Lord's presence in new ways. Writing, and responding in writing to our reading, can be transformational.

Private writing is not expensive. It is not hard. It is simply a matter of knowing some fundamental principles and putting them into practice.

The people who, throughout history, have changed the world for Christ include men and women from different races, different family and socioeconomic backgrounds, different branches of the faith, different areas of expertise. Some were old, some young; some were slaves, some prisoners, some free. They are an incredibly diverse group. But a common denominator is writing: almost to a person, they wrote privately. Could it be that their writing helped them to hear God, to set goals and to persevere in giving their lives to sacrificial service?

The men and women who are considered our spiritual heroes were private writers—letter writers, journal keepers, diarists. Jim Elliot, Amy Carmichael, David Livingstone (missionaries); Queen Victoria, William Wilberforce, Abigail Adams (godly men and women in politics); St. Augustine, Martin Luther, Jonathan Edwards, John Wesley and C. S. Lewis (great thinkers and paradigm shifters) all wrote privately.

Moses, mentioned over six hundred times in the Bible, wrote the Pentateuch (Genesis through Deuteronomy) as well as the lyrics to songs (see Exodus 15:1-21, Deuteronomy 31:30—32:47) and poetry (Psalm 90). David, called the "man after God's own heart" (Acts 13:22), wrote seventy-three of the psalms—his private writing shared publicly. I think it is possible that God used Moses' and David's writings to transform their lives before they were used to transform ours.

Men and women down through the centuries have found the process of writing immensely profitable. I believe God has created us to benefit from purposeful writing, both writing that is private and writing destined for a public audience. Not all of us will publish, but all of us can benefit from writing to reflect on our lives and on the Scriptures in order to live in ways that please the Lord.

Why do we need to write? Recent technological advances have sped up our productivity. Even so, we don't seem to have gained extra leisure time for reflective practices. Instead we've added more activities. Our full schedules squeeze out times of reflection. Unless we purposely plan time to reflect, we probably won't. Unlike Jesus' disciples, we don't have the daily opportunity to take long walks down dusty roads and enjoy early morning fishing trips. While people in biblical times traveled from town to town, fished and farmed, they had time to think. Our after-school carpools and bumper-to-bumper commutes don't naturally lead us to ponder a thought. And our worlds are often noisy: CD players at our workstations, radios and televisions in our kitchens, cell phones and pagers in our pockets. Unless we make it a priority, we may never sustain thoughtful reflection or focused inquiry. It's rare for many of us to spend even fifteen minutes a day pondering a question, assessing where we are headed or responding to a passage of Scripture.

Private writing gives us the time we need to pause and consider our lives. It gives us time to think, to grow closer to God.

In today's culture we spend little time *really* writing. We no longer write personal letters. Most of us depend on telephone conversations or quick e-mails, maybe a quick thank-you note, to stay connected. We don't often pick up a favorite pen and spend an hour or two carefully choosing words to express our heart or share our life. In the past, many women in Western cultures wrote privately: "they wrote letters, . . . they kept diaries, and they recorded important family events in Bibles and daybooks."[4] While previous generations wrote and accumulated trunkfuls of letters, today women no longer have that responsibility.

Unless we make a point of writing, we miss the discovery aspect of writing. When else do we stop to think about what we feel for someone? Taking the time to identify and express our hearts is profoundly important. How else will we discover what we truly appreciate about someone, or the significance of day-to-day events, if we don't pause long enough to think about them? Previously this happened naturally as people wrote letters. Today, even though we are immersed in a world of words, we may never write thoughtfully ourselves. The speed and availability of electronic communication is radically changing how we keep in touch. While we are gaining efficiency, we are losing the regular habit of pausing to consider our lives as we write.

A year or two may pass without any personal record of significant milestones. We move quickly from one experience to the next, and if we don't write down our lives, within a few weeks our memories fade and we forget. We can become disconnected even from our own life experiences. Most of what we think about is what will happen next; what remains in our memories are our most painful or shocking experiences. We forget the small kindnesses of friends, answered prayers, victories we achieved, concerns that the Lord took care of. One of the key reasons we need to write is that it keeps us mindful of our spiritual journey and the people and insights that shape us along the way.

When we write, we make what we are learning our own. James Britton calls this "expressive writing";[5] it is our personal expression of what we are thinking as we try to understand something for the first time. Writing helps us to make the connection between what we already know and what we are trying to learn.

Tom Romano, a well-respected author and teacher of composition, writes, "Teachers in every discipline must come to realize that writing is not merely a means of communicating messages. They must understand 'that writing is basic to thinking about, and learning knowledge in all fields.'"[6] Writing, I believe, is at the heart of our learning. Therefore it makes good sense to write in our journals about what we are learning about our life with God and the Scriptures. Writing about what we are studying helps us to understand it and incorporate truth into our lives. Some educators go so far as to say that writing may be "*the* major instrument for learning."[7] Why do we write? We write to learn.

Why We Don't

You may be thinking, *But I hate to write.* Of course you do. Given the way writing is typically taught, it's a wonder anyone likes to write.

I still remember feeling devastated one afternoon in second grade, almost forty years ago. My teacher returned my paper with a large red D right in the center of the top margin. Throughout my printed text, she had circled five lowercase *a*'s. Instead of simply touching the beginning point as I completed the initial circle of the letter, I had overlapped the lines. Mrs. Taylor hated overlap. I felt terribly ashamed as I took my paper to her desk and asked if this meant I would get a D on my report card.

In my elementary school, and possibly in yours, "writing" was synonymous with "handwriting." If you had messy handwriting, you may have grown up thinking you could not write well. Yet obviously, perfect penmanship has little to do with quality writing.

My husband remembers spending hours writing a college essay only to receive an F on form. This was before the days of spell-check, and he had misspelled *existence* seven times in his paper. One spelling error, repeated seven times, was grounds for failure.

Writing is sometimes judged by accurate spelling. If you could not spell, you may have grown up thinking you could not write well. Perfect spelling has everything to do with editing, but little to do with writing. I've heard President John Adams quoted as saying that it's a darn poor mind that can think of only one way to spell a word. In fact in previous generations people (including Shakespeare) sometimes signed their names three or four different ways. Poor spelling does not mean that you cannot write well—it just means that you need to run spell-check before you publish. And no one will be checking the spelling in your private journal.

The vast majority of us have some negative experience connected to writing. Students often conclude that teachers grade papers against a secret standard known only to them. We believe they don't necessarily teach us how to write, but they still expect us to hit their imaginary mark. When we don't, the comments can be devastating. Tom Romano remembers, "My essays were always messy with the instructor's markings, rhetorical questions, and at least one devastating, incisive comment that made me take the grade I'd received and run."[8] It is extremely embarrassing to have tried to write a great paper yet completely failed. Unless the years of humiliating comments were counteracted by a teacher who encouraged us, we may still have negative feelings about writing. No wonder we don't like to write.

Did you have teachers who assigned sentences as disciplinary consequences for misbehavior? If you were a particularly mischievous child, you probably wrote them by the thousands: "I promise that I will never again chew gum in class." No wonder some of us experience writing as punishment. It was.

And it's not just school experiences that make us feel negative about writing. Recently I asked some college students to write what they felt when I said "diary." One young woman wrote: "When I heard *diary*, I felt bad about writing." A young man wrote, "Diaries make me feel regretful." I am not sure why these students felt this way. Maybe they kept a diary during very painful times growing up. We too may hesitate to begin a journal because we have some residual negative feelings from the past.

"But I Can't"

There are many reasons we feel that we can't keep a journal. You may think that to keep a journal you must write daily. If you really aren't good at daily disciplines—in fact, you haven't found time to read your Bible daily—why would you begin trying to keep a journal? The good news is, it's fine if you don't write each day. Who can? Give up the notion that to keep a journal you must write every day. Instead, decide to write when you are able.

Maybe you've always wished you could keep a journal, but you think only people who are real writers can make good use of one. Writing isn't an innate gift. Well, maybe "great writing" is, but few of us are aspiring to be the next Hemingway. We tend to assume that people sit down and write publishable prose in their first attempts. But most great writers actually revise their writing ten, twenty, thirty times before it ever gets to the published page. I've heard that Hemingway revised the last page of one of his books thirty-nine times. There is so much more to writing than the shine of the final product.

So we may think that we can't write when actually the teacher was grading our handwriting or our spelling. We may be afraid to write because writing feels really risky or full of drudgery. We may resist writing in a journal because we aren't the "daily discipline" kind of people. All of this can change as we experience the transformational power of writing.

If we live very full days and rarely experience true silence, and do not have the habit of writing personal letters that would give us a chance to pause and reflect, when do we ever stop long enough to evaluate how we are doing? When do we keep watch over our heart? When do we monitor our closeness to Jesus? When do we assess our motivation? When do we evaluate whether our behavior lines up with our convictions? Keeping a journal provides us with the opportunity to give attention to all of these things.

It's possible to get so focused on living day to day that we never reflect on whether all of our activity is heading toward the right goal. Are we growing closer to Jesus? Are we listening to the Lord and obeying his Word? Are we putting first things first? If we aren't crafting a soul, paying attention to *our* heart, who is?

Solomon begins Proverbs with this godly warning, a bit stronger than Anna Quindlen's but to the same point: *we* are responsible to open ourselves to the Holy Spirit, to pay attention to our heart and nurture our soul:

> *Wisdom calls aloud in the street,*
>> *she raises her voice in the public squares;*
> *at the head of the noisy streets she cries out,*
>> *in the gateways of the city she makes her speech:*
>
> *"How long will you simple ones love your simple ways?*
>> *How long will mockers delight in mockery*
>> *and fools hate knowledge?*
> *If you had responded to my rebuke,*
>> *I would have poured out my heart to you*
>> *and made my thoughts known to you.*
> *But since you rejected me when I called*
>> *and no one gave heed when I stretched out my hand,*
> *since you ignored all my advice*

and would not accept my rebuke,
I *in turn will laugh at your disaster.*" (Proverbs 1:20-26)

Are we so busy with trivial pursuits that we have ignored Wisdom's warnings? If we seek the Lord, responding to his call, he makes his thoughts known to us. If we ignore Wisdom and go on our merry way, we fall into foolishness by our own choice.

The great news is that the choice *is* ours. We are the ones who decide if we will keep diligent watch over our heart and seek the Lord or if we'll ignore him. Journal keeping can help us to embrace wisdom, respond to the Lord and grow deeper in relationship with Christ. I hope you will take the risk and embark on the journey of private writing. What do you have to lose?

GETTING ORGANIZED
Considering the Possibilities

... So that everyone may see your progress.
1 TIMOTHY 4:15

W̲hat kind of writing would you like to do? There are various kinds of private writing: diary, journal, memoir, autobiography. Each has its own particular focus. For instance, a *diary* is usually a chronological, day-by-day or week-by-week record of what happens in our lives. A *journal*, on the other hand, records private observations—reflections on life or focused inquiry into a topic. *Memoirs* is a term linked to remembering; memoirs look back on life experience from a very subjective point of view. *Autobiography* captures key experiences throughout life and may develop important themes such as movement from childlike innocence to adult maturity or sinner to saint.

Personal letters can also be generally categorized as private writing.

Sometimes each entry in a journal is a letter, even though the writer has no intention of ever mailing any of them. Some letters are written to an intimate friend, someone who knows us so well that we feel comfortable being as transparent as if we were writing for ourselves. So even though these letters are shared, they aren't public. Letters can be formal or informal, but they are distinguished by the fact that they are written to a specific person. The letter writer chooses words and develops her ideas with this person or group of people in mind. A journal might be structured as letters written to God or to one of our children.

As you begin your journal, think about how you are going to approach it. Maybe you would prefer to keep a diary or write your memoirs. Maybe you want to journal about your spiritual progress. As I look through what once were blank books but are now filled with my writing, I find diary entries and memoirs as I recorded a memory from childhood or college days. But for the most part my blank books are journals; I primarily write observations, reflection and inquiry for the purpose of enjoying the Lord, growing spiritually and learning. Why do *you* want to write?

Beginnings

Often I am asked how I organize my journal. While there is no "right" way or even "best" way to organize a journal, seeing how someone else has organized theirs expands the possibilities for us to consider when organizing our own.

I have organized journals in different ways over the years. Usually I start at the front and at the back of my blank book simultaneously. The first page is always the title page. There I write the date that I begin the journal and leave space to write the date that I finish writing it. I also note who gave me the blank book, if it was a gift. I might give my journal a name (in 1974 it was "Idea Trap" and in 1997 "Quilted Hearts"). I sometimes leave several pages blank in the front, so that I can go back at the end of the year and create a table of contents as I reread the journal. It usually takes me a year to fill up a blank book.

Some years as I begin a new blank book, I divide it into sections, simply by folding over the upper corner of the page that begins each section. Each section is essentially a chapter. One section is for lifelong dreams and goals, another for chronological entries. One is for Bible study reflections, another for sermon notes. These sections are followed by various lists in the back.

At the front, after the few pages saved for a table of contents, I write my lifelong dreams, copied from my previous journal. These include dreams for travel, career, personal experiences and lifetime accomplishments. I note progress toward these goals and make adjustments. I also copy annual goals from last year and set new goals for the coming year. These usually fall into the four categories found in Luke 2:52: "And Jesus grew in wisdom [intellectual] and stature [physical], and in favor with God [spiritual] and men [social]." I set goals for what I want to learn during the coming year. I also think about my health and appearance and set some physical goals. I consider my spiritual life and set some goals for Bible reading, ministry and disciplines. Finally, I consider my friendships and determine how I will strengthen them and grow socially. I set goals not only for myself but often for my children as well.

Middle Sections

I typically begin writing chronological entries following these front pages. I begin most entries with the date (month, day, year) and often the place, if I'm not home. I'll sometimes record the passage of Scripture I've been reading. I may note what else I've been reading. Whatever writing I do during the time I set apart to spend with God goes in this section—including response to passages of Scripture.

Sometimes I note the key insight from my entry in the upper margin of my journal. Sometimes I wait until I'm rereading my journal after Christmas to make these margin notations. Doing some form of indexing helps me to find important passages and key insights later on.

I'm usually working through a longer section of Scripture or a book of the Bible, and I save a section toward the back of my journal for these Bible studies. Here I write down my dialogue journaling (discussed in a later chapter) and notes from commentaries, dictionaries and encyclopedias. I might do a word study. I might brainstorm questions to ask my small group.

Notes I take during sermons are sometimes recorded in a separate section. But sometimes I record them among my chronological entries. I know it's risky taking my journal to church, but I hang on to it pretty tightly. There have been times when I kept a second notebook for sermon notes. When I write while I'm listening, I find I listen better.

Lists in the Back

In the back I keep a section for "prayer requests for others." This list may move chronologically backwards beginning on the last page. I don't generally keep long lists to pray through. My recording of prayers is mainly to help me remember names or circumstances, so that when I pray throughout the day, if I don't remember a specific request I can look it up. Sometimes I write my own prayers here. I also like to copy down the prayers of others from Scripture or the Book of Common Prayer or other books. I may write a prayer for my husband or children that will serve as a model prayer for me to pray for them for several weeks.

I may set aside a small section for thoughts regarding a committee or board that I'm on, or a page for ideas I want to keep in mind as I teach Sunday school or lead a Bible study. I often start a section to record ideas from a book I'm reading or a tape I'm listening to.

I often have pages devoted to ongoing lists: books that are recommended to me, websites, short-term goals or weekly tasks. I might keep a page for writing down what the Lord says to me during a sermon, which is different from the usual notes I take. Recently I've been comparing and contrasting the world's values with Christ's values—an evolving list that I'm adding to throughout the year. I've also found it encouraging to keep a list of specific ways I've seen the Lord work in my life.

There's really no right way to organize your blank book. My way is simply functional for me; it allows me to go back into that journal a year or two later and find what I'm looking for. Some years I had so many sections going that I needed to number the pages and create a table of contents as I wrote. Other years this wasn't necessary.

The most important principle is to just begin. You may begin writing with a deep desire to write your family history and halfway through want to write something else. Write what you feel like writing. As you do, you'll find you don't want sections, or you do. Create as you go, and at the end of the year you'll have a better idea how to organize the next year's journal. Organization is a dynamic process. Simply begin, and make the necessary adjustments as you go.

3

STEPPINGSTONES
Principles to Follow

I love those who love me,
and those who seek me find me.
PROVERBS 8:17

The many benefits of journal keeping are available to all of us. Writing privately is not really hard. It is mostly a matter of knowing some fundamental principles and putting them into practice.

Plan to Keep It Private
Many of us, I think, harbor a secret desire that what we write will be admired by others. For my journal to be really helpful to me, I had to give up this fantasy. A journal needs to be private.

No one is going to read the pages of my journal but me. In fact, I have a joking agreement with my dear friend that should I die, she will burn all of my journals. And my husband, children and I have a solemn agreement: we don't read each other's journals. Ever. I know that my journals will never be published. They aren't for my children. They are my *private* journals.

I have some "godly woman" journals I don't mind if others read. In them I copy favorite passages and write out prayers. I also have started journals for my children, with pieces of family history and family anecdotes I love. But my working journal is private. I might choose to read something in a public setting that I've written in my journal, or draw from my journal for an article I'm writing, but I certainly don't write in my journal thinking it will one day be public.

You may want to talk with your spouse, children or roommates and secure an agreement that they will not read your journal. If you believe they might read it, lock it up in your file cabinet or hide it. If no one is going to read your journal, then you are free, free to be bare-naked honest. If your journal is private, there is no way to fall short of expectations of what a godly person ought to be. Once you settle in your heart that no one will read your journal, that it will never be given to your children or grandchildren, you can get serious about the process of transformation.

If you want to keep a "godly" journal, or a journal to pass on to the next generation, you can keep two journals: one private, one public. But don't compromise your ability to work things through with the Lord because you are harboring the thought, the hope, the fear that someday your journal will be read by your family or best friends or even published. Right from the start, plan to keep it private.

Have No Fear of Failure

Your journal is like mine if it contains your journey. Some of what is written is wonderful, and some of it is heresy. It takes awhile to distinguish the flowers from the weeds. Somehow, thankfully, the Lord uses the mess to help us grow to spiritual maturity. There is no such thing as journaling well, or conversely, journaling badly—unless you are not honest. Because there is no right way to journal, there is no way to fail.

No one else will ever need to see the mess. If no one reads our journals, then no one will judge our ability to write or spell or use commas. They won't be judging our character either. What we write in our journals doesn't have to be final thoughts; journals are not intended to be conclusions. Final thoughts belong in our books; these are our journals—our first-draft stuff. First drafts are meandering, exploratory expeditions. We don't have to write complete sentences, set the entire historical context or balance every thought. Jesus knows all of that. We want to get to the crux of the matter, follow our developing thoughts, push our thinking further. We'll sense where we need to begin. We don't need to worry about telling the whole story.

We can work hard to be specific. We can take time to pay close attention to details and to our emotions. When we sense an emotional response, we can pursue it. As Ralph Fletcher reminds us, that's what our journals are for. "It gives you a roomy space to record and explore what amazes, delights, disgusts, or appalls you."[1] Because our journals are private, we are free to be absolutely candid. No one's looking over our shoulder. We cannot fail.

Journaling Takes Time

Writing takes time. But it doesn't have to take a *lot* of time. Even fifteen minutes is beneficial. Reflective writing may actually save us time if it clarifies our thinking so we make a wise decision. Writing can keep us from wasting weeks in mental anguish nursing a grudge. It can keep us from throwing away years of hard work, as it did for William Wilberforce (see chapter four) when he was being tempted to leave behind his lifelong work to abolish slavery in the British Empire. Writing will take time, but *not writing* may take more. Writing is time well spent.

Journaling takes time if we plan to write as we read books or the Scriptures. Obviously reading goes much more quickly if no note taking or responsive writing is involved. But I have found that such writing keeps my thoughts focused. While I'm writing I can think more deeply about what I am reading, probing it from various perspectives. If I write as I read or think, my mind stays focused. As I'm crawling along, I find insights I don't find when I read at a normal speed. Give yourself time to reflect on what you read, and as you read, write down your thoughts.

The Choice Is Yours

There are no formulas—I don't always write first, then read, then conclude with a prayer. I do what I sense I need to do each time I sit down to have my quiet time. Spontaneity helps me to avoid getting into a journaling rut. Sometimes I don't write at all. Sometimes I don't write as I read. I think of my journal as a tool I use for what I need that day.

There is no prescribed way to journal. I get to choose how I want to use it, how I set it up and what topics I'll write on. No one should dictate these things to me. It's my journal. It's my choice. It's just for my use.

Minimizing Worries

At times I sit down to be with the Lord and I am so overwhelmed with stress and anxiety that I can't focus. My mind keeps jumping back to my worries. Or a million tasks come to mind. When I feel like this, before opening my Bible I may jot down a list of what's bothering me. A recent list started like this:

☐ Mail check to Erin
☐ Call AWANA girls
☐ My future career direction

☐ Ants in the yard

☐ Need shoes

☐ Library books are due

It went on and on. Looking it over, I could then figure out a plan: what I could do today, what I needed to talk with my husband about, what phone calls I needed to make. As long as these concerns rumbled around in my thoughts, I worried about them. Once I wrote them down, they were no longer overwhelming, and I could determine what could be taken care of and what would need to be left alone for the time being.

If as I am reading the Bible or praying a new worry comes to mind, I can quickly add it to my list. There it will be kept safe for later attention.

Rather than making a bulleted list, sometimes it's good to write for ten minutes about particular concerns. Besides tasks and worries, strong emotions can distract us. Teacher Peter Elbow finds that ten minutes of "freewriting" often helps students clear their minds to focus on a writing task. Freewriting (writing, nonstop, whatever comes to mind) can keep powerful emotions from distracting us when we intend to write. "Sometimes your mind is marvelously clear after ten minutes of telling someone on paper everything you need to tell him. (In fact, if your feelings often keep you from functioning well in other areas of your life frequent freewriting can help: not only by providing a good arena for those feelings, but also by helping you understand them better and see them in perspective by seeing them on paper.)"[2] Use your journal to clear your mind of mental and emotional distractions.

Guard Your Freedom

So as you begin to keep a journal, commit yourself to keeping it private. Don't worry about failing: no one will ever see it. No one will know how regularly you wrote in it. No one will know how sloppily you wrote. No one will know if you didn't use standard spelling and punctuation. Feel comfortable giving yourself time to reflect on life and consider what you are reading. Feel free as you stand at the helm charting your own course, day by day. Consider using lists or freewriting to help you deal with distracting thoughts and emotions.

Above all else, begin. Don't put off growing deeper in your love for God. Only you, by God's grace, can listen to Wisdom calling and craft a life for your soul.

J STROKES
Staying on Course

So, if you think you are standing firm, be careful that you don't fall!
1 C O R I N T H I A N S   1 0 : 1 2

I like to spend time on Sunday mornings looking back over what I've done during the previous week. Sometimes I've been so busy that I didn't sit down with my journal at all. I then spend time looking at all the activity and bring it before the Lord and acknowledge that I've given my time to worthwhile things. I may realize that I gave time to some not-so-worthwhile activities as well.

This examination of my life helps me to keep on target. I don't go too long without evaluating whether I'm giving my time to the things that are truly important to me. I also use this time to check off the goals I've accomplished and to set new goals for the week.

Press Meaning into Your Week

I learned from William Wilberforce the importance of regularly spending time reassessing my direction. Gordon Macdonald writes:

William Wilberforce, a committed Christian, was a member of the English
Parliament in the early years of the nineteenth century. As a politician he
was noted for his vigorous leadership in convincing Parliament to pass a his-
toric bill outlawing slavery in the British Empire. It was no mean feat. In
fact, it may have been one of the greatest and most courageous acts of states-
manship in the history of democracy.

It took Wilberforce almost twenty years to construct the coalition of law-
makers that eventually passed the anti-slavery measure. It required detailed
documentation of the injustices and cruelties of slavery, persuading lawmak-
ers who did not want to offend the interests of big business, and standing
strong against a host of political enemies who would have loved to see Wilberforce fall. . . .

The central issue of the day in England was peace; Napoleon was terroriz-
ing Europe, and the concern was whether or not England could stay out of
war. Wilberforce was rumored to be among the candidates for a cabinet post,
and because of the peace policy he found himself most anxious to gain the
appointment. Garth Lean, one of Wilberforce's more recent biographers, tells
the story.

"It did not take long for Wilberforce to become preoccupied with the possibility of the appointment. For days it grabbed at his conscious mind, forcing
aside everything else. By his own admission he had 'risings of ambition,' and
it was crippling his soul."

But there was a disciplined check and balance to Wilberforce's life, and in
this particular situation that routine became indispensable. As Lean says,
"Sunday brought the cure." For there came a regular time in Wilberforce's
private world every week when he rested.

The Christian politician's journal tells the story best, in its entry at the
end of that week of furious fantasizing and temptations to politic for position:
"Blessed be to God for the day of rest and religious occupation wherein
earthly things assume their true size. Ambition is stunted."[1]

Macdonald continues:

*Thus, rest is not only a looking back at the meaning of my work and the path
I have so recently walked in my life; but is also a refreshing of my belief and
commitment to Christ. It is a fine tuning of my inner navigational instru-
ments so that I can make my way through the world for another week. . . .
We affirm our intentions to pursue a Christ-centered tomorrow. We ponder
where we are headed in the coming week, month or year. We define our
intentions and make our dedications.[2]*

Certainly rest—stopping our usual activity to focus on Christ—
will help us to focus our lives. For me, writing these reflections
helps to crystallize my thinking.

The J Stroke

Recently I was at a technology convention, and one of the speakers
mentioned that the space shuttle is off-course 99 percent of the
time. Computers continually have to trigger the rockets to fire in
order to make small adjustments and keep the spacecraft headed
toward its destination.

My husband learned the same principle as an Eagle Scout, canoe-
ing the lakes of the Pacific Northwest. If two people paddle a canoe,
even if they are on opposite sides of the boat, the leverage of the person in the stern is stronger, causing the canoe to go around in cir-
cles. That is why it is impossible to keep the canoe heading straight
across the lake—unless you use the J stroke. With the J stroke you
momentarily use the paddle as a rudder: looking at the canoe's current direction, looking at the landmark where you are headed, the
person in the stern uses a J stroke to realign the canoe with the goal.

Like the space shuttle and the canoe, the only time we are
entirely on course is during that brief time when we are crossing
center on our way back off course. We too need the J stroke to get
realigned.

A regular time for realigning our activities with our goals is important if we hope to reach a particular destination. Looking back on our previous week and looking forward to the week ahead, remembering the bigger picture and what we hope to accomplish, helps us to stay aligned. In this time we may pat ourselves on the back and say, "Good job." No one else may recognize our efforts, and others may take the credit for our ideas and the good things we've contributed. When we affirm ourselves, we don't need to get public recognition. We can do our good works in secret and look forward to the applause of God in eternity (Matthew 6:5-8).

RETURN
Revisit Your Journal

Your love is like the morning mist,
like the early dew that disappears.
HOSEA 6:4

It has been helpful for me to reread my journal periodically throughout the year and again after I've completed it, to see the broad brushstrokes of the Lord's hand in my life. I usually have extra time during the week between Christmas and New Year's to spend a couple of hours rereading my journal.

As I reread, I see areas of growth and am reminded that I have been struggling with some things for the whole year. I find that in the passages where I'm pouring out my soul or passionately articulating my side of an argument, I often don't seem very mature. It's OK because no one is going to see these rantings, but over the years it has helped me realize that the thing that upsets me so terribly right now will probably not be such a big deal by next January.

I am filled with gratitude to read through lists of prayer requests and remember all the Lord has done. As I read through my reflections in Bible study, I may find ideas that seem brand-new. Obviously they are not, but over the year I forget a lot. Rereading helps me to remember. Remembering is important.

Remembering the Lord in Prosperous Times

The book of Isaiah contains a tragic reminder of how quickly we can forget God. After all the miracles God performed on behalf of Israel, and all the prosperity he blessed them with, they forgot him. "You have forgotten God your Savior; / you have not remembered the Rock, your fortress" (Isaiah 17:10). The Lord loved his people and desired a relationship with them, but their love had grown cold. They had become infatuated with other gods. The Lord says to them that they have become an adulterous wife (see Jeremiah 3:6-20; Ezekiel 16). Those words have haunted me.

In Hosea, the Lord says it again: "Your love is like the morning mist, like the early dew that disappears" (Hosea 6:4). I never want to hear Jesus say that to me, yet I know how prone I am to fall in love with everything else in my life. It is so easy to take for granted the faithfulness of God's love for me. It seems that prosperity was the Israelites' spiritual downfall—they began to take credit for their good fortune and success. Their ancestors had fallen into the same trap. So do I.

A thousand years before Isaiah, Moses expressed concern that when the Hebrew people settled into the Promised Land, they would forget the Lord:

When you have eaten and are satisfied, praise the LORD *your God for the good land he has given you. Be careful that you do not forget the* LORD *your God, failing to observe his commands, his laws and his decrees that I am giv-*

*ing you this day. Otherwise, when you eat and are satisfied, when you build
fine houses and settle down, and when your herds and flocks grow large and
your silver and gold increase and all you have is multiplied,* then your
heart will become proud and you will forget the LORD your God,
*who brought you out of Egypt, out of the land of slavery. . . . You may say to
yourself, "My power and the strength of my hands have produced this wealth
for me." But remember the LORD your God, for it is he who gives you the
ability to produce wealth, and so confirms his covenant, which he swore to
your forefathers, as it is today.*

*If you ever forget the LORD your God and follow other gods and worship
and bow down to them, I testify against you today that you will surely be
destroyed.* (Deuteronomy 8:10-19, emphasis added)

In the desert, each day, the wandering Israelites had to trust the
Lord for food. In the land flowing with milk and honey they
wouldn't *have* to trust. And they didn't. How quickly they forgot.
Moses' worst fears were realized. As for their descendants during
Isaiah's time, prosperity was their stumbling block. Why should we
assume *we* are immune to the dangers of prosperity?

The writer of Revelation addresses Jesus' words to another
wealthy generation of believers. Their good fortune also blinded
them—they didn't think they needed God. "You say, 'I am rich; I
have acquired wealth and do not need a thing.' But you do not realize that you are wretched, pitiful, poor, blind and naked. I counsel
you to buy from me gold refined in the fire, so you can become rich;
and white clothes to wear, so you can cover your shameful naked-
ness; and salve to put on your eyes, so you can see" (Revelation 3:17-
18). These are timely words for us as well.

Our self-sufficiency can rob us of a heart that is tender toward
Jesus. I have to ask myself, Am I a spiritually adulterous wife? Is my
love like the morning mist? It's better to face the truth today than to
go on my heedless way until disaster strikes, or I stand before the

judgment seat of Christ and realize my stupidity: I forgot the Lord. Jesus gives us the solution: "So be earnest, and repent. Here I am!" (Revelation 3:19-20). Our protection against the snare of prosperity and the deceitfulness of wealth is *repentance*. We need to regularly make an assessment of our hearts, an honest assessment, and repent. Then we turn to Jesus and invite him in. He says he is standing at the door knocking. We can throw the door wide open and let him in.

I use my journal to write about my relationship with the Lord and to remember he is the one who is blessing me. Every good gift is from him (James 1:17) and not my own doing. I also write my repentance so I'll have a record of it and remember his grace.

Built-In Reminders

I've read through Exodus, Leviticus, Numbers and Deuteronomy and made a list of all the ways God built reminders into the law. I was amazed at the number of them. I've tried to build in reminders for myself and our family as well. Saying grace before every meal can be a meaningless ritual, or it can be a built-in reminder that God is with me and an opportunity for me to quickly reaffirm my love and trust in him.

Jesus established a new sacrament, Holy Communion. He wants us to remember his love: "Do this in remembrance of me" (Luke 22:19).

Our son fell off a ladder and broke his arm when he was nine. The doctor told us the nerves might be severed. He might lose the use of his hand. We prayed. The nerves weren't severed, just trapped in the break. Jeff recovered. We wanted to remember and celebrate as a family how the Lord protects us, so from then on every year on the anniversary of Jeff's surgery we reenacted our drive to the hospital, paused to thank the Lord for his care for us throughout the year, and then went out to dinner. This ritual became a part of our family tradition, a built-in reminder of the Lord.

As I write, I try to think about ways to build in reminders for myself throughout my journal. I don't want the important insights to be lost. I don't want to forget those times when the Lord is so real to me. I don't want to forget my helplessness or how I am "prone to wander." So I mark the page, or create a list, or copy a verse onto a 3x5 card. I may write an invitation to Jesus to come into my life, to sit down and have dinner with me. These invitations can be reread and prayed again.

Taking Care

The apostle Paul recognized this need for paying attention, for being careful, for remembering the failures of those who lived before us and being warned. First, he writes to the Corinthians that he is driven to run hard so that he will not be disqualified from winning his heavenly reward: "Do you not know that in a race all the runners run, but only one gets the prize? Run in such a way as to get the prize. Everyone who competes in the games goes into strict training. They do it to get a crown that will not last; but we do it to get a crown that will last forever" (1 Corinthians 9:24-25).

Am I running in such a way as to win? Am I in strict training as an athlete, or am I running aimlessly, simply boxing the air? These are great questions to try to answer in my journal.

But Paul's exhortation to the Corinthians continues. He reminds them that the Old Testament (specifically the Exodus-Deuteronomy period) is full of people who didn't finish well. He says that their stories and their consequences are written for us as a *warning*. "So, if you think you are standing firm, be careful that you don't fall!" (1 Corinthians 10:12). Be *careful*.

How do we take such care? The stories of the Old Testament

saints should cause us to take seriously the need for assessing our direction and making adjustments. The more regularly we realign ourselves, the easier it is to get back on course. I don't just want to run hard, I want to qualify for the prize.

You may want to consider how you can set aside a regular time to assess your direction and decisions in light of your goals. Your journal time on a chosen day of the week can be devoted to making an assessment, so you can make small directional adjustments to align yourself with your destination.

Take advantage of the rich record contained in your journal. Schedule time to go back and reread what you've written during the month or over the course of the previous year. Our journals can help us to be careful, so that we run well all the way to the finish line and qualify to receive the prize (2 Timothy 4:6-8).

6

PEARLS AND SNAKESKINS
Our Preparations

In his heart a man plans his course,
but the LORD *determines his steps.*

PROVERBS 16:9

Janet, a friend of mine, always gets out her favorite string of pearls when she plans to write. Ron has to wear his baseball cap. Hemingway began each morning with a certain number of sharpened pencils.

Writing rituals help us begin. I find that routine ways of beginning help prepare my heart not only for writing but for reading and praying as well. Having a beginning ritual helps us to leave distractions behind and to focus. Ever watch a professional baseball player approach the plate? What you are watching are beginning rituals.

Often as I sit down at my desk, I am surprised that I feel ready to talk to the Lord and to listen. I think this readiness comes at least in part from my starting at a fairly consistent time of day, in a usual place and in a routine way. It is important to give some attention to the way you begin.

When we moved to San José, it took awhile for me to reestablish my favorite routines. I like to have a special place, my familiar journal and my pen. Sure, I can journal without these, but I like having them. I bring them with me when I travel. They help me begin.

Your Special Place

The wife of a professor at Dallas Theological Seminary told me she had a large Queen Anne armchair in her living room where she always sat when she prayed. One evening she sat down in her chair when friends were visiting. Suddenly she realized she had tuned out the conversation and was completely lost in prayer! Sitting in the chair put her in a praying state of mind. It was her praying place.

For fourteen years I sat on the left side of our living-room couch in Los Angeles, facing the front door, for my devotions. It really didn't disturb me if the children ran in and out; when I was in my place I could focus. But since we moved to San José, that place on the couch is no longer my spot. We still have the couch. It still faces the front door. But it's not my spot. I don't know why—but it isn't.

Now I like to sit at my desk in the guestroom, surrounded by my books. I smell my fresh cup of coffee and warm my hands on the mug. I look at my pen and remember. I look at the cover of my journal and feel the paper. Often I hear Canada geese honk as they fly overhead. These rituals are my string of pearls. This is how I like to begin.

Ralph Fletcher, one of my favorite writers and a teacher of writing, keeps photographs, artifacts from childhood, rocks, owl pellets and a snakeskin by his writing desk. Yes, a paper-thin snakeskin. He writes: "I have a snakeskin from a garter snake pinned to the wooden frame of the window above me. I love its translucency and lightness. . . . The snake decided he no longer needed it, but I do. In its way it tells me: Risk everything. Outgrow yourself."[1] That's what journaling is about. Outgrowing ourselves—growing beyond the borders of our current thinking, beyond our comfort zone, growing as lovers and seekers. Journaling is recording the journey, taking note of the various skins we shed as we are transformed into the image of our Savior.

The walls in my room have artifacts that are meaningful to me: my diploma, a few AWANA awards, a thank-you note from one of my students, pictures of trees I have loved.

Creating a spot can be as simple as gathering your Bible, journal and pen, along with a few books or cassette tapes in a basket placed next to your favorite chair. Or maybe you can collect what you need in a book bag. Maybe the computer is your journal. Wherever it is, create a safe place, free from knocks on the door and the ringing telephone if possible, a place where you can put out a "do not disturb" sign (at least metaphorically), and begin.

Rearrangements

Unfortunately life's not always routine. For several weeks I had known that my husband would be gone on a particular Monday. I looked forward with great anticipation to a leisurely morning with the Lord, reading and writing. I got the children off to school, made a fresh pot of coffee and walked into our guestroom; my heart had been anticipating this time and it was prepared to begin. But my children had "played office" in my place. My books were scattered. My papers had been rearranged. The children's books, pens and stickers lay all over my desk, the floor and the bed. I opened a drawer—it was filled with envelopes and junk mail retrieved from the wastebasket. My place was in such a mess that I could not begin. I had totally lost my devotional frame of mind. So I needed to clean up the room and try to begin later.

Now I'm working full time, so my morning routine is not nearly so leisurely. I use my desk for work (preparing to teach, grading papers) and a few creative endeavors. I've discovered the hard way that I need to clean my desk the night before so it is prepared, free of distractions for the morning. If not, I may waste my devotional time attending to something else that catches my eye.

Maybe, unlike me, you need your desk to be piled high in order to settle in and concentrate. You can't work unless you're surrounded by a mess—that's what you need to begin. Whatever your personality, be sure to give some care to how you begin your writing time. Developing some habits, some beginning rituals, can help prepare your soul to meet the Lord.

Your Paper and Pen

Sometimes I am asked what kind of a blank book I use or what I think about journaling on a computer. For years I wrote in the cheapest blank books I could find. A few years ago my sixteen-year-old son bought me a journal with a cover photograph of a little boy holding out a long stemmed red rose. I loved the picture and how it symbolized his love for me. Last year he bought me another. This year a new friend unexpectedly bought me a blank book with a different cover illustration: large clusters of grapes in Swedish blue and yellow, symbolizing joy and fruitfulness—we serve a congregation with deep Swedish immigrant roots. So these last few years my journals have been an unexpected gift of love.

It doesn't really matter what kind of a journal you choose. Most of mine have had lines to write on, but some haven't. Those without lines invited me to draw or create a poem spontaneously. The paper in some of my journals is really wonderful, but most isn't. Recently I've been learning about bookbinding. I think it might be fun to make my own blank book with just the right textures and colors of paper.

There are lots of varieties of blank books. Just choose one that feels right and will last.

For years I journaled with any pen I could find. Now I often use a special pen—a gift from a mentor/professor/boss who placed his trust in Christ just weeks before he went to Germany for cancer treatment. Against the odds, he returned home healed. "Every teacher needs a Monte Blanc," he told me. The pen reminds me that the Lord hears our prayers for wisdom and healing, and it gave me encouragement to pursue my dreams to teach even when all the doors to teaching seemed shut. After being out of the classroom for three years, I was asked to teach again. My pen reminds me: God answers prayer. I also have a box of pens with different colors of ink and some calligraphy pens. My collection is growing with time.

David Livingstone, a medical missionary to the Cape of Africa, gave his life to outlawing the slave trades. He also mapped much of the southern portion of Africa. His lifework changed England. Writing was an integral part of his life, but blank books were not always readily available. "When Livingstone ran out of notebooks he sewed ancient newspapers together and wrote across the type in ink made from tree juices."[2] So the paper and the pen we use really don't matter; it's the writing that counts.

Margaret Guenther, an ordained Episcopal priest and seminary professor, writes that she prefers binders to blank books. "By keeping the journal in looseleaf binders, I am able to write on the typewriter or word processor and to include letters, poems, and articles that have become part of my story. Journal entries can be made at any time and any place, then carried home to be placed in the binder."[3] Using binders may be a great idea for you.

I personally have a hard time using anything other than pen and paper for my journal. Something doesn't feel right when I try to journal at the computer. The creative aspect of reflection is somehow stifled when I'm typing. Maybe it is because typing is too fast, so I don't have the time to think as I do if I'm hand-writing. Maybe typing is associated with work and school for me. But this is not true for everyone. Many journal keepers love using a computer. It's up to the writer to decide; certainly we are not limited to a small blank book and a fountain pen.

At times what I wanted to write wouldn't fit in a book. So I bought a huge piece of paper (24 x 36 inches) and created a poster. Last year I wanted to record my journey of discovering what Moses had done that caused God to keep him from entering the Promised Land. After all the times God had been ready to destroy the Israelites and start over, I couldn't figure out what was so offensive about Moses' hitting the rock rather than speaking to it. Why would God keep him from leading the people across the Jordan (Numbers 20:1-13; Deuteronomy 3:21-28)? Was God really fair in keeping Moses out of the Promised Land? Was he just? My study led me to other passages of Scripture and to many other places (including literature of the Holocaust), and as I read I wrote on the poster paper. The answer to the fairness of Moses' discipline seemed to be found in the holiness of God. As I read commentaries and articles in Christian magazines, the theme of holiness stood out. These authors were helping me come to some conclusions. Each time I gained a new insight into the holiness of God, no matter where it came from, I added it to my poster. After several months the poster filled up. It's a wonderful visual reminder of my study, and all of the Aha! moments are on one page, wonderfully easy to recapture.

Give attention to the aesthetics of your place, your journal, your pen. Surround your writing place with meaningful remembrances and images of what you strive to be. Establish some beginning rituals. Use these simple tools to help your heart and mind begin.

HONESTY
Our Commitment

He ... who speaks the truth from his heart ...
will never be shaken.
PSALM 15:2, 5

J ohn Steinbeck observed in a letter to Peter Benchley that "the written word punishes both stupidity and dishonesty."[1] This is true. When we read what someone else has written, places where logic breaks down or the words don't ring true stand out. Unfortunately we don't always read our own writing with such objectivity because we are too close to it. Often it is not until we reread our journal entries a month or two later that we have a degree of objectivity.

Write Honestly

In our journals we seek to write honestly. But as all writers know, it's not always easy to admit the truth, let alone write it. We are trained to be polite. As Ralph Fletcher notes:

[We] *find it almost impossible to be totally candid, even when we're writing*
for our own eyes only.

    I'm not immune to this problem. Rereading my notebooks I come upon
page after page of writing that is superficial, worthless, dishonest. Even when
describing a painful family situation, I tend to "make nice" and write in a
cheerful or impartial voice instead of banging on the table and screaming
like I want to. These are the places where I fail myself: the real stuff of my life
never gets written down.[2]

In our journals we benefit the most from honest writing, from
pausing to close our eyes to select just the right word to pinpoint
our thinking. We may not fully know what we think, but through
honest, specific, written expression we usually find a developing
clarity of thought. It serves no purpose to avoid the truth. Write candidly, even if you are not proud of the attitudes or lack of character
that are revealed on the page. Perceiving our flaws can be the beginning of change.

    Some of us are unaware of our flaws and the reasons we do what
we do. J. P. Morgan observed that "there are two reasons why a
man does anything. There's a good reason, and there's the real reason." Many of us look at how we live our lives and think we're
doing OK. We haven't hurt anyone or abused our kids. I'm afraid
we deceive ourselves. John writes to Christians, "If we claim to be
without sin, we deceive ourselves and the truth is not in us" (1
John 1:8). Sure, some of us keep all of the religious rules: we don't
swear, steal or kill. But righteousness in God's kingdom lies
deeper, in motives.

    Our heart's motivation matters to God. True righteousness is
not just about what we don't do. True righteousness is about why
we do what we do. In our journal, we have the opportunity to
reflect on what is really motivating us. *What is going on within my*

heart? Our hearts are at the core of our motivation. "From the heart arise unknowable impulses as well as conscious feelings, moods, and wishes. The heart, too, has its reasons and is the center of perception and understanding. Finally, the heart is the seat of the will: it makes plans and comes to good decisions. Thus the heart is the central and unifying organ of our personal life."[3] When we write in our journal, we seek to uncover the motivation from which our actions and decisions arise.

A Heart's Deceit

As Jeremiah makes clear, it is our heart that deceives us into thinking that we are pleasing God when we are not. Our motives may be hidden from our perception, while God sees them (Jeremiah 17:9-10).

It may be useful to consider why we pretend we are "more godly" than we really are. We are often the last to know how full of envy we are. We may not even realize that we are angry, bitter or mad at God. Instead we smile. We want people to see that we are trusting God.

We can think we are trusting the Lord and serving with pure motives when in fact we are depending on our own capabilities and serving because we think we will earn God's approval. How do we get beyond the good reasons we so easily generate to the real motives lurking under the surface? If we are masters at deceiving ourselves, how do we ever have eyes to see the truth?

Journaling can help us to see our own heart as God sees it and repent. In our journals, if we can come to understand more deeply the love of God and the grace Jesus shows to us sinners, we begin to see ourselves as we really are.

Consider taking half an hour to write down all the reasons why the Lord would not be pleased with you. *What motives lurk in your heart?*

We are all a mess. The good news is that Jesus loves us and forgives us if we simply come to him in repentance and faith. We have no need to deceive ourselves. The more we perceive our depravity and our need for Christ's forgiveness, the more grateful we will be for his love. His grace invites us to love him with all our hearts.

Being Forgiven Much

Viewing ourselves as righteous actually has quite a downside. Simon the Pharisee had convinced himself that he was righteous. Like all good Pharisees, he fasted twice a week and gave a tenth of everything, even a tenth of his spices. He knew the Scriptures. But in comparison to a woman who knew the depth of her depravity, Simon didn't love. Jesus said to Simon:

> *Do you see this woman? I came into your house. You did not give me any water for my feet, but she wet my feet with her tears and wiped them with her hair. You did not give me a kiss, but this woman, from the time I entered, has not stopped kissing my feet. You did not put oil on my head, but she has poured perfume on my feet. Therefore, I tell you, her many sins have been for-* given—for she loved much. But he who has been forgiven little loves lit-tle. *(Luke 7:44-47, emphasis added)*

The depth of our love is in direct proportion to the extent that we grasp the depth of our sin and God's grace toward us. In our journals we have the opportunity to get real before God, to reflect on how much we've been forgiven, and to fall deeply in love with the Savior.

Once we come to terms with the truth of the motivations of our heart and realize Jesus loves us even though we're a mess, our spiritual life will never be the same. We are Simons, critical of others, satisfied with ourselves. Yet Jesus loves us! Comprehending our depravity and his love for us nonetheless, letting the truth of these doctrines permeate our hearts, can begin as we journal and reflect.

You may want to take one of the following steps. And as you do, ask the Lord to reveal to you what's in your heart.

☐ Take an hour and reflect in your journal on how self-sufficient you've become, how little you actually depend on God in prayer, how full of pretense you are.

☐ Read through the Gospels; when you come upon Jesus' rebukes of others, ponder whether he might say those same words to you today.

☐ Keep an account of how faithful you actually are to your spiritual disciplines.

☐ Copy passages of Scripture that express God's love for you, even when you didn't deserve it.

☐ Study the life of Peter.

☐ Read more about Paul's doctrine of grace.

Writing honestly about what is going on inside me is the first step toward living authentically. If I can't be honest with myself, I won't be honest with others. Don't be discouraged if as you reread your journal you realize that you didn't go deep enough into your *true* feelings or thoughts. Renew your resolve to write candidly, to bang on the table, to be honest with yourself. Our journals can teach us, over the years, to be more honest—to see our shortcomings and sin, and to change.

INTIMACY
Our Goal

Love the LORD *your God with all your heart*
and with all your soul and with all your strength.
DEUTERONOMY 6:5

In the 1600s Francis de Salle wrote a very simple yet profound guide to living a life devoted to Christ. One of his key principles is to pay attention to what is going on inside our hearts: "What kind of love have you for your own heart? Are you not willing to serve it in its infirmities? Alas! you ought to assist it and procure assistance for it whenever passions torment it, and for this purpose to neglect every other consideration."[1]

With his encouragement in mind, I often begin my quiet time with my journal open and quickly take an assessment of my heart. Do I feel close to Jesus? Do I want to write for a while to explore why I'm feeling a little distant? What assistance does my heart need? What struggles is it experiencing? What sin remains unconfessed, what anger unresolved? I may want to write; I may not. If I do write, as I conclude my thoughts I'm usually writing a prayer.

Even if I'm feeling close to the Lord, sometimes I don't feel like opening up to his Word. So I need to "procure assistance" for my heart. Rather than ignore my feelings, I write. What assistance does my heart need? I may read something besides the Bible—a devotional, a Christian author, a non-Christian author, poetry, stories, anything that may help me to warm up a bit. Sometimes I quickly ascertain that I don't need to begin with writing. I open the Bible and read a passage that I've been studying for a while, or begin in a new place. If I feel like it, I write a responsive dialogue with the Scriptures.

The purpose of beginning this way is to be intentional about loving the Lord and not letting my devotional time become rote and detached from passion for him. As Dallas Willard encourages us, "We must purposefully, humbly and intelligently cultivate the ability to listen and see what is happening in our own souls and to recognize therein the movements of God."[2] Cultivating an awareness of the state of my heart is an essential reason for beginning my devotional time with writing. Learning to purposefully listen to God and perceive his movements is crucial as well.

Taking a spiritual assessment, taking time to confess my sins and failures, writing, reading, studying, meditating, memorizing and praising are for the purpose of drawing near to the Savior. This devotional time usually leads me to an internally quiet place. I simply sit and embrace the love of God. No guilty conscience. No sense that I haven't done all I should have. He loves me and I enjoy sitting quietly in prayer, with or without words, simply being in his love.

Transitions and Nosegays
From this quiet place I try to move gently into "noisier" things,

meeting deadlines, attending to tasks. When there is time, I sometimes walk a little to transition from my devotional time into my day. Even if I don't have the option of a gentle transition, I love to savor a little of the sweetness of my time with the Lord throughout my day. I may take a new insight, a verse, something from my devotions to carry with me. Francis de Salle calls this a nosegay. I envision picking a little bouquet of fragrant rosebuds to carry out of my secret garden. Their sweetness can bring me back to the quiet place even in the midst of a hectic, interrupted day.

This nosegay may not be anything I could describe to others without sounding trite. It may be something that I've known for years, but for some reason it came alive for me in a new way. It is best kept to myself, tucked away in my journal and hidden in my heart. A secret, just between the Lord and me. Actually, sharing these thoughts with others can leave me feeling spiritually cold. Talking about them somehow dampens my passion. I don't understand why this is. Usually our impulse is to share with others the new things we've seen. But sometimes we may need to keep them to ourselves. The desert fathers thought that sharing thoughts from private times with the Lord was like leaving a barn door open—words, they felt, let the heart's passion out.[3]

Being Near

My goal during my time with Jesus is not to find profound thoughts. That may happen, but that's not my intention. I remind myself that I am *in his presence*. I seek to worship him from deep within my soul. I open my heart to him and his Word and ask him to draw me to himself. I seek to nurture my soul in him.

Jesus offers us the gift of himself—his love, his peace, his forgiveness, his comfort, his wisdom, his guidance. In my journal, as I reflect on his Word, I receive his gifts and offer him the gift of myself. My gift is my love and my life, available to be used by him however and wherever and for as long as he chooses. During my devotional time, I want to deepen my comprehension of his love for me and to reaffirm my devotion to him. Writing helps me make him my One and Only and remember that I live my life before an audience of One.

Here I find no place for duty or obligation—I'm with him because I love him, not because if I don't spend the next twenty minutes having my devotions he'll be mad and punish me. Writing helps me draw close to him. Don't let journal keeping become an obligation or a discipline that keeps you from reaching your real goal.

Our love for Jesus, our worship, our writing to grow spiritually must not degenerate into mere rule keeping. This is the trap the Israelites fell into during Isaiah's time. They went through the motions of keeping fasts and keeping the sabbath, but they had lost passion for the Lord. He rebukes them: "These people come near to me with their mouth and honor me with their lips, but their hearts are far from me. Their worship of me is made up only of rules taught by men" (Isaiah 29:13).

We can use reflective writing to help us keep our hearts tender, open, in love with the Lord. Our journals can help us assess the state of our hearts, the degree of warmth that exists between us.

Reflect on your heart's condition; run to its assistance if necessary. Be on the lookout for duty and obligation sneaking in to reduce your worship and Bible study to mere rule keeping. Use reflective writing to purposefully, humbly and intelligently seek the Lord.

Part 2

UNCOVERING THE PROCESS

So to walk, even as he walked . . .
1 JOHN 2:6 KJV

A Best Friend
Discovering Our True Feelings

I have called you friends.
JOHN 15:15

Sometimes we do not have the wonderful safety of a true friend. There have been times when I couldn't share my hurts or struggles with my Bible study group because I was the pastor's wife and most of my struggles were with the pastor or the others on staff or the people in the church. It wouldn't have been right to work through my frustrations in this context.

So I turned to the privacy of my journal, and it in essence became my best friend. I was safe with my journal. What I wrote would never be seen by anyone else; it wouldn't make the circuit and come back to be used against me, or be twisted and misunderstood. It would never hurt anyone. In my journal I don't have to be balanced or weigh words carefully. I just pour it all out, then reread what I've written and try to understand why I'm so frustrated.

Sometimes there are other reasons we don't feel comfortable sharing our struggles with others. A few months after we moved to San José, my husband made a comment that puzzled me. Instead of arguing with him or denying the validity of his observation, I spent some time writing. I reflected on his comment in my journal as if I were out having lunch with a friend:

> *Kevin said that I don't seem happy. Is it staying home? The pressure of not enough money? Not having a car? No real friendships? No one who truly knows me and values my friendship? Everything is so surfacey—no one knows my character—just my position. No real affirmation. No depth from which to have a significant relationship or a significant conversation. I can't see that I'm able to minister at all. Three months of cleaning house and pleasant conversations and concern over the boys wanting to go back to L.A. and not living in a "neighborhood" and overhearing implications about what people think about our neighborhood and the horrendous house prices so that we'll never own our own home. Ashley has no friends on the block to play with—ugh!!!*

Until Kevin said those words and I journaled about them, I didn't know I was not happy. I didn't even know these frustrations were piling up, robbing me of joy. But as I explored the possibility that I was unhappy, the words poured out. Kevin was right. Looking at what I wrote, I realized that I was under a pile of struggles. I was stressed. No wonder Kevin noticed something wrong.

Upon reflection it seemed reasonable that these things would weigh on me. I was hitting the wall, almost going through culture shock, which is pretty typical after moving. Women in our new church didn't need to hear me whining about all this. My husband really didn't need to hear it much, either. I didn't have a best friend to talk to. So I used my journal over the next few weeks to sort things through—and eventually my joy returned.

One purpose for keeping a journal is to have freedom to share our burdens even if we don't have a trusted friend. As we write conversationally, we shed light on what's going on within us.

Journaling in this way also helps us to be free to truly listen to others. Often I do not feel a need to do a lot of talking because I've done my "talking" in my journal. So I'm free to truly listen and *be* a best friend.

If you need a trustworthy best friend, a place where you can speak your mind without having to be a blessing, a place where you can pour out your heart and someone will listen, a place where you can be honest about your shortcomings and sin, maybe you will find, as I have, that as you wait for trustworthy friendships to develop, your journal can be a wonderful, listening, safe, best friend.

THREE LIGHTS
Discovering the Voice of God

Therefore, consider carefully how you listen.

LUKE 8:18

W e have this promise in James:

> *If any of you lacks wisdom, he should ask God, who gives generously to all without finding fault, and it will be given to him. But when he asks, he must believe and not doubt, because he who doubts is like a wave of the sea, blown and tossed by the wind. That man should not think he will receive anything from the Lord; he is a double-minded man, unstable in all he does. (1:5-8)*

Those who have placed their trust in Jesus have the privilege of seeking wisdom from the Lord, and while we wait for his wisdom, we have the responsibility of maintaining our trust confidently in him. We don't want to be vacillating between belief and doubt.

I write in my journal to monitor where unbelief has crept in. I also write to discern God's voice and to perceive the wisdom he is giving me through the Scriptures, the Holy Spirit and others.

The Scriptures

What is God saying to me in my study of the Scripture? We must be careful not to use the Bible as a fortune cookie, taking verses out of context and believing that God has given them to us in order to make a decision for us. We cannot read the verse "Go and do likewise" (Luke 10:37) and take it to be God's will that we start a new business. Verses are not personal crystal balls, predicting the future, promising prosperity. Likewise, we cannot take a biblical figure of speech and apply it literally—"If your left eye causes you to sin, pluck it out." Sound interpretation of Scripture is required if a conclusion is to have biblical authority. We must do our best to present ourselves to God "as one approved, a workman who . . . correctly handles the word of truth" (2 Timothy 2:15). Our journals are wonderful tools for doing careful, thoughtful Bible study.

As we study the Scriptures, journaling can also help us to hear God speaking to us, giving us wisdom as we make a decision or seek guidance. Of course it is very possible that God has already revealed his will and he has nothing new or specific to say to us. Then our journals help us to apply what we already know to the situation.

When you hear God speak, write it down. Dallas Willard encourages us to have a regular plan for listening to God.

Listen, carefully and deliberately, for God. When God does speak to you, pay attention and receive it with thanks. It is a good habit to write such things down, at least until you become so adept at the conversational relationship that you no longer need to. If he gives you an insight into truth, meditate on it until you have thoroughly assimilated it. If the word he has given concerns

action, carry it out in a suitable manner. God does not speak to us to amuse
or entertain us but to make some real difference in our lives.[1]

Have a place in your journal where you regularly, routinely capture
the truths God speaks to you through Scripture.

The Holy Spirit

A second important way we hear the Lord is through the inaudible
voice of his Spirit speaking in our thoughts. So in my journal I write
down my reflections and what I've been thinking about. I seek to be
open to hear the Lord speaking to me in his still, small voice, not
just for decision-making but also for teaching and correction that I
may become more like Christ.

Listening to God in prayer and listening to the truth he whispers
to us are important aspects of growing deeper in our life with God.
This voice is not outside of us but is heard in thoughts that come
from the Spirit who dwells within us.

Some thoughts we might identify as coming from our conscience, leading us to be uncomfortable if we are considering doing
something we know is wrong. Some thoughts highlight something
we did that was hurtful; they rightly lead us to ask someone to forgive us and to turn to the Lord for confession. Some thoughts
prompt us to take action, to do good. As we are praying, we have
thoughts. All day long we have thoughts.

Are all of our thoughts "God thoughts"? I don't think so. The Lord
says, "My thoughts are not your thoughts" (Isaiah 55:8), so we know
that we don't naturally think about life the same way that God does.
Not every thought that comes into our mind is a God thought. We
must be discerning.

Some thoughts that come under the guise of conscience are not
from God. For instance, we may have a false sense of guilt after a

loved one dies—unwarranted guilty thoughts that are not true and therefore not from God. We may hear voices that say we are not good enough for God to love us. Such thoughts are lies—they contradict the truth of Scripture. Distinguishing between our thoughts and God's thoughts takes discernment and careful attention.

How can be we begin to discern what God is saying to us? How can we listen to his voice? Writing down the thoughts we have is very helpful, because writing helps us to discern which thoughts are lies. Sorting through our thinking to determine what is true and what is false can take place in our journals. Writing often brings clarity.

While we are learning to recognize God's gentle whisper to us, we can write down what we think he has said. God's voice always speaks words of truth and never contradicts his written Word. If we compare what we think we heard God say to what he has revealed as right and true in the Scripture, we can more objectively discern his true voice.

Others

A third way we hear the Lord is through conversations we have with others. It's not uncommon for the Lord to speak through a comment a friend makes, a note someone sends, a radio talk-show guest, a conversation over dinner. If we meet regularly with fellow believers, often without knowing it they will speak a word from God to us.

Recently I was asking the Lord for wisdom as I prepared a message for a women's retreat. In passing, a friend said, "Wow! That must be hard to boil everything you have to say into an hour."

Actually I was wondering how on earth I was going to talk for sixty minutes. But as she said that, I knew she was right. It was as if God himself had spoken to me. I was trying to put more and more into my talk to fill the time. Instead I needed to focus. I needed to settle on one main idea, not fifteen. I made sure to write my friend's words in my journal, because God had spoken through her to answer my prayer for wisdom.

Later that day my husband was reflecting on his own sermon preparation. He mentioned that Donald Barnhouse said we don't prepare a message, we preach "out of the overflow." *Aha!* Another word from the Lord for me. I needed to relax and share with the women out of the overflow of what the Lord was doing in my own life. Again, I got my journal and wrote it down. In fact I began to compile a list of what the Lord spoke to me about preparing messages.

Sometimes God speaks to us through the godly counsel of a friend, a pastor or a mentor. Sometimes we hear God most directly in what we hear *ourselves* saying.

Three Lights Together

From these three lights (as previous generations have called them)—study of Scripture, the Holy Spirit's whispers in our thoughts, our conversations with others—we may see common themes emerging. When all three are pointing to a common truth, we should pay attention.

Journaling is a great way to gather all that we are hearing from these different sources. We can then come to some conclusions about what we believe the Lord is speaking to us. As always, we must remember our heart's potential to be deceptive. As Willard cautions, sometimes we do not hear accurately. God may be speaking truth and we may be missing it, or hearing it wrong.[2] The value of writing is that we can bring what we think we're hearing into the light. We can talk about it with others and ask the Lord to show us if we are hearing correctly.

We might begin a journal entry listing the main themes we are encountering in Bible study. Does a particular word seem to be jumping off the pages? A few months ago it seemed that every place I read, the word *repent* showed up. So I wrote in my journal awhile, asking the Lord to show me what I might need to repent of. I noticed that I was trying to be in control, to take charge. I didn't know what it meant, but I was aware of it. Then on Thursday night during our small group Bible study, instead of understanding a friend's lack of spiritual vitality, I said something to try to "fix" her. As soon as the words were out of my mouth, I knew the Lord was showing me something. Later, when I journaled, I realized that he was revealing my need to repent of self-sufficiency and renew my dependence on him. I finally saw how my Bible study, my thinking throughout the week and a conversation with others were all pointing to this one area of my life. I discerned that the Lord was speaking to me. It was time to listen.

We should be careful not to lean too heavily on our "leadings," or on the counsel of others, and think we have an infallible word from God. We may be misunderstanding him. We must be humble and discerning. What we do know is that God would never lead us contrary to his revealed will in the Bible (for example, he would never lead us to enter into an adulterous relationship). Since we are fallible, subject to being deceived by our false motives, it seems prudent to look for God to give us wisdom through a *composite* of all that we are hearing. F. B. Meyer, writing in the early 1900s, cautions against leaning too heavily on our feelings or inner thoughts without the balance of the truth of God's written Word:

> A subtle danger, taught by some earnest people, is to magnify the inner light and leading of the Holy Spirit to the neglect of the Word which He gave, and through which He still works on human hearts. This is a great mistake and the prolific parent of all kinds of evil. As soon as we put aside the Word of God, we lay ourselves open to the solicitation of the many voices that speak

within our hearts. We no longer have a test, a criterion of truth, a standard
of appeal. . . .

   We must not content ourselves with the Spirit without the written Word
or with the Word without the Spirit. . . . The Word is the chosen vehicle of the
Spirit. Only by our devout contact with it are we able to detect His voice. It is
by the Word that the Spirit will enter our hearts.[3]

Spending time recording what we are hearing in our journal over the course of several days or even weeks can help us to truly listen to God. We can then share all we've gathered with our spiritual director or trusted friend and glean his or her understanding. The wisdom we receive from these three sources, however, does not make a hard decision for us. We prayerfully discern the truth, and then it's up to *us* to decide.

11

FINGERPRINTS
Discovering the Lord in Nature

When I consider your heavens, the work of your fingers . . .
PSALM 8:3

I like to use my journal to capture times when I see the Lord. I often see him in nature—so I write. Abraham Lincoln did too: "I never behold them (the heavens filled with stars) that I do not feel I am looking in the face of God. I can see how it might be possible for a man to look down upon the earth and be an atheist, but I cannot conceive how he could look up into the heavens and say there is no God."[1]

I want to live with eyes to see what Lincoln describes as the face of God. I love to look at nature and see God. I don't actually see him, but I know he exists because I see his fingerprints on each tulip, and I learn about him as I watch the ocean pound the shore just as it has day after day from the beginning of time.

The seas have lifted up, O LORD,
  the seas have lifted up their voice;
  the seas have lifted up their pounding waves.
Mightier than the thunder of the great waters,
  mightier than the breakers of the sea—
  the LORD on high is mighty.
Your statutes stand firm;
  holiness adorns your house
  for endless days, O LORD. (Psalm 93:3-5)

Paul tells the Romans that each of us is responsible to believe there is a God and know his divine attributes because he has revealed himself to us through his creation: "For since the creation of the world God's invisible qualities—his eternal power and divine nature—have been clearly seen, being understood from what has been made, so that men are without excuse" (Romans 1:20). In our journals we can embrace God's revelation of himself to us through all he has made.

A tree in winter spoke so powerfully to Nicholas Herman (Brother Lawrence) that he gave his life to Christ. A friend, M. de Beaufort, recounts their conversation of August 1666:

He told me that God had done him a singular favor, in his conversion at the age of eighteen.

  That in the winter, seeing a tree stripped of its leaves, and considering that within a little time the leaves would be renewed, and after that the flowers and fruit appear, he received a high view of the providence and power of God, which has never since been effaced from his soul. That this view had perfectly set him loose from the world, and kindled in him such a love of God that he could not tell whether it had increased during the more than forty years he had lived since.[2]

That tree had stood there for years, silently testifying to the glory of God, a living metaphor of the providence of God. Many people had walked by without noticing. Maybe even Brother Lawrence had walked by the tree many times without seeing. But this day he had eyes to see the "providence and power of God" on display.

Louisa May Alcott, at the age of twelve (1843), writes in her diary about experiencing God in nature:

> I had an early run in the woods before the dew was off the grass. The moss was like velvet, and as I ran under the arches of yellow and red leaves I sang for joy, my heart was so bright and the world so beautiful. I stopped at the end of the walk and saw the sunshine out over the wide "Virginia meadows."
>
> It seemed like going through a dark life or grave into heaven beyond. A very strange and solemn feeling came over me as I stood there, with no sound but the rustle of the pines, no one near me, and the sun so glorious, as for me alone. It seemed as if I felt God as I never did before, and I prayed in my heart that I might keep that happy sense of nearness in my life.[3]

When Alcott was in her fifties, she looked back at this entry: "I have, for I most sincerely think that the little girl 'got religion' that day in the wood when dear mother Nature led her to God.—L.M.A., 1885."[4]

We can miss the face of the Lord, we can miss seeing his fingerprints all over our world, if we don't live with our eyes wide open. We need the Lord to help us see. In our journals, as we try to capture the living metaphors of nature, we see. Sometimes we see so intensely it's as if we have eyes to see heaven. When we see evidence of God all around us, it confirms our faith that he is here, present, with us. We are not alone (Matthew 28:20).

I write to capture the wonder of God's transcendence when his presence is especially vivid to me. I sat by the river that over the years had carved out Kings Canyon, and I wrote:

I stand in awe, seeing the utter beauty of the pines and brilliantly blue skies, and I worship within. My whole being is lost in reverent devotion to the Lord God. Now, giving him my all, all my own hopes and desires, my plans and dreams, my entire life, my health and husband and children, my finances, my schedule, everything is gladly given to him. How totally ridiculous not to. Nothing is of any worth except knowing him. How odd that just two weeks ago I was desperately struggling to regain my eternal perspective after only a few days away. Now, loving and worshipping God in my center, with undivided attention and devotion, is so easy, so natural, the only sensible response to his creation. Oh, dear Lord Jesus, ruler of all creation, Almighty God, Everlasting King, you alone are worthy of all my love and undivided devotion now and forever.

As I write and reflect on these experiences, they fill my soul and draw me into worship. Then during spiritually dry spells or periods of doubt, I can reread and remember that the Lord truly is here, even though I don't sense him right at the moment.

Earth's crammed with Heaven,
and every common bush afire with God,
but only he who sees takes off his shoes.

ELIZABETH BARRETT BROWNING[5]

12

EYES WIDE OPEN
Discovering God in the Usual

For in him we live and move and have our being.
ACTS 17:28

I write to be aware of the Lord in the daily happenings of my life. If I didn't write about them, I might miss his involvement in my life.

Our move to San José sparked a new interest in hospitality, and for a time I reflected in my journal on being hospitable. Because I was writing about this, I became particularly aware of demonstrations of hospitality. I noticed references to hospitality in Scripture and in conversations. The Lord was speaking to me about welcoming others through various means.

Thinking this morning about hospitality, the role of preparing a place for others—creating a sense that they are welcomed and valued, set at ease. Not putting them off with fancy stuff, but extending a wel-

come through unexpected thoughtfulness. I want to be that kind of a hostess, even as a Sunday School teacher welcoming new students, and a pastor's wife. May everyone who comes to church or comes into our home sense God's love. Father, help me to love you wholeheartedly, not with reservation or self-consciousness but freely, extravagantly devoted to you . . . even in my service and giving time to make special preparation for others. Thank you for welcoming me into your home and for going to prepare a place for me. Amen.

This reflection led me to think about Jesus' hospitality as he prepares heaven for us, which led me to John 14:2: "In my Father's house are many rooms; if it were not so, I would have told you. I am going there to prepare a place for you." Later that week I went to a friend's home for a board meeting, and the way she invited us into her home touched me deeply. Sitting in the airport, waiting for my flight home, I wrote:

Dear Ginger,

Once again I leave your home so full—your love for me demonstrated in so many little kindnesses this weekend has refreshed my spirit. Your time preparing the Saturday food and agenda—your attention to the beauty of your guestroom and bath—your thoughtful questions and listening ear. Where else would I find a friend like you?

As I sit in the airport waiting for my flight I'm grateful for your ministry. How absolutely incredible it is to watch each woman grow. The healing and new life in one. Jackie's perseverance and commitment to continue teaching the Word. Others finding joy in their service. Your leadership has made such a difference in all of their lives as well.

I'm taking your example with me as we begin this new ministry. I'm trying to be a leader who sees each woman's potential and prays.

By the time I boarded the plane, I knew what had stirred me in Ginger's home. Her thoughtfulness in preparing and listening communicates love. It frees us to share our struggles honestly and to find encouragement to keep taking risks and growing. The Lord showed me that hospitality, welcoming people, isn't just "being nice"—it is an essential aspect of leadership, and God uses it to build healthy community among believers.

Because I was reflecting on hospitality in my journal, I was awake to lessons about hospitality in the course of daily life. I was able to notice Ginger's example—though I didn't know just how it had touched me until I saw my words written on the page.

Journaling can help us anticipate that the Lord is speaking to us all of the time through our circumstances, interests, friends, what we read, what we hear. And then we are much more likely to see and hear him.

GO WEST!
Discovering New Insight

Now devote your heart and soul to seeking the LORD your God.
1 CHRONICLES 22:19

We write to think. We don't just write to record what we already know. Our thinking develops as we write—we generate new thoughts and extend our knowledge in new ways as we put our words on paper.

Typically our minds are full of feelings, perceptions, images and prejudices that are not specifically named or categorized. While the chaos swirls without words or logic inside our heads, there is confusion. The irrational carries as much weight as the rational. It can be hard to evaluate what we think with any degree of objectivity until we see it written down. Writing forces us to define our feelings with words. Once we do, we can work to understand them. We write to find insight into ourselves, to generate new thoughts, to order the chaos. In essence, we write to discover what we think.

The process of writing generates new insight. Students often don't think they have anything to write about until they start to write—and then they discover aspects of their topic they had never really thought about. I've heard novelists say that they don't know what a character will do until they write her into a scene. In fact author Anne Lamott says, "Writing a first draft is very much like watching a Polaroid develop. You can't—and, in fact, you're not supposed to—know exactly what the picture is going to look like until it has finished developing."[1] Our journal writing is a first draft. We don't know what it all adds up to, but we will, if we allow it to develop. We need to keep writing, exploring, discovering and seeking to understand, because eventually we will.

Assigning words to our feelings is the beginning of understanding them. The vast majority of our emotions and thoughts are not particularly meaningful, but as we consider what we've written, something of great significance may begin to take shape. Maybe tomorrow we'll begin with the emerging image, asking the Lord to show us the way. This generative aspect makes journal writing an adventure. A good question is often the starting point for the journey.

Questions to Ask Ourselves

How's my walk with God? I write out this question in my journal and then seek to answer it honestly. I wonder, *On a scale of 1-10, how's my walk? How close do I feel to the Lord today? Why?* A number will come to mind, and I write it down. Then I explore the reasons I think I feel like an "8" instead of a "10." *Do I feel like God is mad at me? What's keeping me from saying my walk with God is a 10? What's been left undone?* I try to keep short accounts: *Do I have unfinished business with the kids or someone at church? Have I been hurt? Am I angry? I* assess the vitality of my spiritual walk.

Why do I want things this way? A seminary professor and clinical psychiatrist, Dr. Paul Meier, once taught us the principle that people don't stay in situations that aren't at some level advantageous for them. We're all too selfish to continue to live in a miserable situation. So if I'm miserable, and staying miserable, I need to explore the possibility that at some unconscious level I am more comfortable with the misery than having the misery fixed. On some level the situation may be serving some need I have.

This principle helps to explain codependency. I've heard stories of women who will complain for years about their alcoholic husbands; yet once the husband stops drinking, the wife shocks everyone by leaving him and marrying another alcoholic! At some level it works for her to be in a relationship with an alcoholic, no matter how truly miserable it makes her.

We write to think outside the box. I ask myself hard questions about possible twisted motivations for my struggles and write out my answers. I discover things that I think, things that I never really knew I believed before I began writing. I ask myself questions that not even a best friend might feel comfortable asking. *Why do you want things to be the way they are? Why did you feel hurt? Where's all the intensity coming from?*

☐ When I'm having a hard time sticking to a diet I ask, *Why don't I want to lose weight?*

☐ When I notice my quiet times are no longer regular and I can think of all kinds of good reasons I can't read my Bible, I ask, *Why don't I want to spend time with God? Did something happen that I wish hadn't happened? Am I mad at him?*

☐ When I'm feeling like others are sucking the life out of me and I don't know what to do about it, I may ask, *Why can't I set boundaries? What's in this dysfunction for me?*

If *you* asked me these questions I'd think you were nuts. Of course I want to lose weight. Of course I'm not angry at God. Of course I don't want to be consumed by my friend. But maybe, just maybe, there's a struggle going on at a deeper level, a struggle that I'm not even conscious of. It's happened so often now that I know it's possible. As I'm pondering the questions, exploring various possibilities, grabbing fleeting thoughts out of the air and writing them down, I sense a response within me that tells me I'm on the right track. I guess I am mad at God. So I *keep seeking.*

Sometimes, it's not the first or second possibility that I explore that really grabs me. But if I stay at it, writing down my thoughts, discovering what's going on inside my heart, I'll write something that rings true. Here is the real treasure.

When you find a shadowy hint of truth, no matter how hard it is to acknowledge, pursue it. Plunge into the murky waters of your heart and search until you find the pearl. Emotion is a neon clue. If a thought brings tears to my eyes, or an *Aha!* response, I know I'm on the right track.

Our youngest son always loved treasure hunts. We'd devise clues leading from the dryer, to the hall closet, to the garage, then under the bed, and finally to what we anticipated would be his favorite birthday gift. One year the clues led all over town before we all arrived at the music store to find his new drum set.

Discovery journaling is a treasure hunt. You uncover a little clue and ponder it. All of a sudden there's a flash of insight and you dash off to the next stop, not knowing if this will be the final stop—the grand finale—or one of many stops along the way. You won't make the big discovery all at once, but if you allow thoughts to unfold, they'll naturally lead you to further thinking, new conclusions—insight.

Structure of Freedom

When we write to explore our thinking, it's best not to have a structure in mind. Structure can thwart our attempts to generate new thought. Mina Shaughnessy has discovered that even in the college classroom, it is crucial not to be too structured in our writing. An outline or a formula can limit us to the realm of what we already think. It's best to approach writing as an adventure and see where it leads us.

According to Shaughnessy, a student is unable to do the most productive thinking if teachers limit

> the freedom of the writer to see and make choices at every step, to move ahead at times without knowing for certain which is north and south, then to drop back again and pick up the old path, and finally to get where he is going, partly by conscious effort but also by some faculty of intellection that is too complex to understand—technique that sacrifices this fullest possible play of the mind for the security of an outline or some other prefabricated frame cuts the student off from his most productive thinking. He must be allowed something of a frontier mentality, an over-all commitment, perhaps, to get to California, but a readiness, all along the way, to choose alternative routes and even to sojourn at unexpected places when that seems wise or important, sometimes, even, to decide that California isn't what the writer really had in mind.[2]

As we write in our journals, we need to cultivate a "go west" frontier mentality and give ourselves freedom to explore bunny trails along the way.

Keep Asking

I left a conference feeling horrible, sure that I had given some dear friends the impression that I didn't want to talk with them. So I wrote.

Why am I so rude? It's the very last thing I want to be, yet I can tell people hear me say in an unintentional comment, in an interruption, in a self-conscious gesture: It's time for you to go now. It's not what I meant. It wasn't even a secret I was hoping to keep. But for some mysterious reason, I do this over and over to my friends. Why?

Kevin thinks it's because I'm embarrassed; my desire is that they will love me, that they will like what I've written or have been helped by something I said, but I wish it didn't matter to me. So I play a game. I tell myself that it doesn't matter if anyone likes my gifts. I tell myself that my gifts are pretty rough and it's embarrassing that they're public. So when someone says something nice—I'm embarrassed. I assume that they are just paying me compliments to be nice. They really don't mean it. I need to let them know that I know that they don't really mean it—otherwise I'm a fool.

So I say I appreciate their kindness and their encouragement, but we all know that what I gave was just OK. After all, I don't want to be the emperor running around with no clothes on! I don't want to be foolish. I guess it's my insecurity that makes me rude.

In this journal entry I sought to know myself. Until I wrote about it, I really didn't know what I thought. I just had some vague feelings that I didn't understand. Writing helped me to define my feelings. If I'm treating people rudely because I'm insecure, then I can begin to work on becoming more secure in Christ and pray that he will change me.

Musings

Sometimes as I begin to write, I recall something I felt or did that puzzled me. Sometimes it's an attitude that I detect underlying a comment I made. Sometimes it's a contradiction. So I reflect on my puzzlement in order to understand it.

Hmmmm

How odd that the slightest critical comment—"the guitar is too loud"; "the sandwiches are cold"; "what a shame to waste so much coffee"— can bring such inner turmoil while 3,000 dead in the earthquake barely disturbs me at all. A distant catastrophe has less impact than a nearby, casual remark. My perspective is too focused on me and how I feel. I am self-absorbed.

Puzzlements provide us opportunities to grow in understanding ourselves. We "put down words with the sole purpose of getting at thinking, at personal truth."[3] We write and suddenly "realize" or "notice" things.

I also write to reflect on what is perplexing to me. When I was struggling with a group I was leading, I wrote, Why doesn't this group seem to be going anywhere? And then I brainstormed possibilities: Is the Bible study guide we're using not meeting their needs? Is the time the problem? the place? Is there something wrong with how I'm leading? When an idea I write rings true, I figure I'm onto something. Most likely it is an idea that hadn't occurred to me before.

Prayer

Sometimes my discovery writing is directed to the Lord—a written pondering in his presence. It could be broadly defined as prayer. Actually it is like many of the psalms. Psalm 76 begins with ponderings and moves to prayer:

> In Judah God is known;
> > his name is great in Israel.
> His tent is in Salem,
> > his dwelling place in Zion.

By verse 4, the psalmist is praying:

You are resplendent with light,
  more majestic than mountains rich with game.

Sometimes (like Psalm 76) my writing does not begin addressing the Lord, yet by the end I'm writing with the knowledge that he's listening. I begin trying to better understand my thinking; then quite naturally my new understanding leads me to pray. Sometimes I don't realize that I'm writing a prayer until I conclude with A*men*.

14

Toward Reconciliation
Discovering the Grace to Forgive

In your anger do not sin.
EPHESIANS 4:26

Sometimes I journal what I really would like to say to someone but can't. I write down my side of an argument. Often I begin feeling absolutely furious or crushed, but by the time I've written it all out I see the other person's perspective and am embarrassed that I was so petty.

I work through the hurts and betrayals of life this way. It doesn't matter whether the offense was intentional or merely a careless mistake. If it bothered me, I need to write about it. Even if the situation would seem like no big deal to others, I write about it if it hurt me. It's hard for me to get beyond my anger if I keep it all inside. Writing it helps me to resolve issues and not spend all my lunches talking with coworkers about my personal problems.

Some people have asked why I write this kind of stuff in my journal. Quite honestly, I sometimes need to talk more than others want to listen. Working through difficult times in my journal gives me a sense that I've been heard—*Jesus has heard*. When I write something down and then go back and read it, I also gain a little objectivity. As long as a troublesome situation remains only in my thoughts, my interpretation of it never has to stand up to the light of logic or a possible alternative explanation. When I reread what I've written, I can see holes in my side of the story.

Journey Toward Resolution

My husband never hurts me intentionally. A slight from him may *feel* intentional, but it is not. He would say that he may be stupid, but he's not mean. It's in the hidden place of my journal that I have the freedom to angrily attack his character and make my case for how he intentionally hurt me. Afterward as I reread what I've written, I can gain a little distance to see how the situation probably looked to him. I begin to understand his perspective, see the misunderstanding, realize that the hurt wasn't intentional and take steps toward reconciliation.

As I enter into conversation with him, the writing I've done helps me to focus my thoughts more clearly. I'm able to explain my perspective; I can listen until I understand his and can take responsibility for where I blew it. Then we can resolve the problem.

The goal of writing is not to build an airtight case so that I can win an argument. The goal is always resolution, the granting of a different perspective, and offering and receiving forgiveness.

Working to resolve conflict in my journal helps me to avoid gossip too. Once I write, I don't have such a need to tell someone all the juicy details of how I've been wronged. My journal writing moves from my very subjective perspective, to seeing my situation in the light of

Jesus' presence, and then into prayer for strength or maturity or whatever I sense I need to resolve the conflict.

Paul urges, "If it is possible, as far as it depends on you, live at peace with everyone" (Romans 12:18). Writing helps me to live in peace with the nice people in my life.

Leaving Room for God

Sometimes peace is *not* possible. Sometimes people intend to do harm and cannot be trusted. Sometimes people are not nice. Paul continues, "Do not take revenge, my friends, but leave room for God's wrath" (Romans 12:19). Many times it would be easy to cling tightly to my hurt feelings, waiting for an opportunity to get even. But revenge, even nonviolent revenge, is never acceptable. If conflicts cannot be resolved, we ask the Lord for the grace to live in unity. Jesus calls us to love everyone—even our enemies. He models for us how to live with difficult people. He shows us how to love them, how to choose not to get revenge. But he also shows us that we do not need to *entrust* ourselves to them. There's a fine balance in loving but not entrusting.

Writing helps me to come to terms with difficult people. I can at least see a reason, a perspective, a difference of opinion, *something* that helps me understand their behavior. I can be humble, seeing their fear and pain, and try to find some reason that it makes sense in their world to be so hateful. It doesn't mean that I come to like them or that my understanding excuses their behavior. I'm not required to bend to their manipulation. Understanding helps *me*: it keeps me humble from the inside as I recognize that in their situation I might be much worse. So journaling helps me work through my hurts and learn how to follow Jesus' example. It leads me to show love and not hostility.

Choosing not to be hostile toward people doesn't mean we don't express hostility in our journals. David wasn't afraid to voice his hostility.

Let not those gloat over me
  who are my enemies without cause;
let not those who hate me without reason
  maliciously wink the eye.
They do not speak peaceably,
  but devise false accusations
against those who live quietly in the land. . . .
Vindicate me in your righteousness, O LORD *my God;*
  do not let them gloat over me.
Do not let them think, "Aha, just what we wanted!"
  or say, "We have swallowed him up."

May all who gloat over my distress
  be put to shame and confusion;
may all who exalt themselves over me
  be clothed with shame and disgrace. (Psalm 35:19-26)

We can complain bitterly in our journals and call down fire from heaven, until we are able to entrust the injustices we've experienced to our holy God and leave room for him to settle the matter.

We write to discover the grace to understand another's perspective.

We write to discover the grace to forgive.

We write to leave room for the wrath of God.

Treasuring and Celebrating
Discovering the Value
of Remembering

Remember the wonders he has done, his miracles,
and the judgments he pronounced.

1 CHRONICLES 16:12

I record significant experiences so I can treasure and remember them. When I reread my journal, I'm reminded of God's blessings and who Jesus is to me.

God's Blessings

Just after we moved to our new home, I hurt my finger and was really in pain as I tried to unpack our belongings.

I had become increasingly disabled by the pain in the joint of my finger in my right hand. After a week of hoping it would get better and a morning unable to wash dishes, sign school forms, put on Ashley's *socks, or make a fist, I sat down and felt discouraged and worn out by the pain. I had a day of computer work and unpacking ahead of me and I didn't see how I could do it. I remembered that I hadn't asked the Lord to take care of my finger—healing it if it was his will. I prayed. Instantly, my pain was gone. My finger instantly healed. God spoke very clearly to me. I am with you! Here! Never before do I remember being instantly healed. God said to me in such a dramatically clear way—I am with you. I hear your prayers.*

Thank you, Lord, for such a clear sign from you. Help me to hold on in faith during long periods of silence and waiting—may I know that you are hearing and are answering in your best timing.

We don't regularly have such incredible experiences when God instantly answers our prayers. When we do, we need to write them down so we don't forget. Even having experienced such a remarkable answer to prayer, God's healing, I forgot. The experience slipped into my long-term memory until I reread my journal at Christmas. Remembering warmed me. *God is near.*

A couple showed remarkable kindness to us when we first arrived at our church. Both worked, and they had taken a week of vacation to put in their new lawn. On the Sunday just after that week, with lots of work still left to do, they drove all the way across town to bring us dinner. We were overwhelmed by their thoughtfulness.

Within a month, however, this couple left our church to begin attending another. When I saw them after that, all I remembered was that they left. The disappointment and rejection associated with that choice completely hid from my thoughts their welcoming hospitality. But as I reread my journal, I remembered their kindness.

Commemorations

I write to commemorate life's milestones. My husband and I cele-

brated our wedding anniversary, and that morning I wrote in my
journal.

On our 22nd Anniversary

*Maybe we're at the halfway mark. Is that possible? So soon? We've grown up
together and we've grown up our children, yet I can still see you in my
mom's kitchen, just 18, and so full of love for me.*

*Your love has been the safety I've needed all of these years. A love that
never rejects though it may be fiery mad. A love that sees past the obvious
and cherishes the potential. A love that warms me when I'm away and welcomes me home. A love that's vulnerable and needs to be loved in return.*

*I fell in love with your character 25 years ago and it has only grown and
matured over these years, blossoming into a heart that knows the pain of
humanity yet holding on to God's gifts of love, mercy, truth, hope, peace, com-
passion, and joy. The bonds of love that bind my heart to yours are stronger
today than ever before.*

*I feel the pain of the inevitable—death will part us—but rather than
recoil in fear of that pain, I want to embrace each day, fully present to our
love.*

Use your journal to treasure life, to celebrate and commemorate
special events, so you don't forget and lose them forever.

16

SEASONED WITH SALT
Discovering How to Make the Most of Each Opportunity

Let your conversation be always full of grace, seasoned with salt.
COLOSSIANS 4:6

Sometimes in anticipation of a meeting, I write down what I'd like to say and what I think the individual's or the group's response will be. This kind of preparation focuses my thinking. Then when I'm actually in the conversation, I know what questions I want to ask and what points I'd like to make.

I've used this strategy when I'm meeting with a woman one on one and want to make sure that our weekly conversations are moving toward a goal. I pray, asking the Lord to show me what he would have us talk about, and I think it through carefully in the morning during my quiet time.

I've also used this strategy as I'm developing a relationship with a non-Christian. I write what I think the Lord might have me say to him that would help him to see Christianity in a new light. I try to anticipate his objections and think through my response in my journal. I've found that there are natural pauses in conversation, and because I've thought through what I'd like to say, I can use a pause to make a transition in that direction. The Lord has used such conversations to draw people to himself.

Writing in preparation is a strategy that has also helped when I'm getting ready to attend a board meeting, especially when we have a difficult situation to address and I want to prayerfully consider our options. Sometimes when I'm feeling stuck, if I take time to write down some possibilities and carry out the thinking to its conclusion, the Lord gives wisdom regarding the problem.

It's not that my mind is made up before I go into a meeting. Quite the opposite, actually. Writing my thoughts ahead of time simply helps me to know what I think, so I can be free during the meeting to hear various perspectives and allow them to inform and possibly change my perspective. As I evaluate others' ideas against mine, questions arise and new concerns come to light. Our collective wisdom helps us find our way toward the best solution.

Do you have a meeting this week where you'll be asked to make an important decision? Do you have a lunch appointment with a friend? Are you worried about a grown child or a roommate, and feel unsure about what to say during your next conversation with them? Take a few minutes to write in your journal, thinking about how you might open the conversation, what questions you'll ask, which thoughts you'd like to express. Maybe the Lord will use your journal writing to clarify your thinking and help you make the most of the opportunity.

A TASTE OF HONEY
Enjoying the Lord

He is to write for himself on a scroll a copy of this law.

DEUTERONOMY 17:18

Before the children of Israel ever thought of having a king, God gave Moses, as part of the law, instructions for selecting a king. God also gave the king a writing assignment:

> When he takes the throne of his kingdom, he is to write for himself on a scroll a copy of this law, taken from that of the priests, who are Levites. It is to be with him, and he is to read it all the days of his life so that he may learn to revere the LORD his God and follow carefully all the words of this law and these decrees and not consider himself better than his brothers and turn from the law to the right or to the left. (*Deuteronomy 17:18-20*)

The king was to write and then read his copy of the law. The king could have been instructed to have the priests or the scribes provide him with a copy of the law, but God wanted him to write a copy *for himself.* Perhaps there is something about the process of copying a text that helps us hear the Lord's word for us personally.

My husband asked me to lead a journaling time during our church's leadership retreat. He'd never asked me to do this before. We anticipated that there would be a lot of resistance to writing. As I prepared, I decided to take the group to the above passage in Deuteronomy. If God wanted the king to copy Scripture, maybe he would have church leaders copy it as well.

So as a team we read the text together and spent a few minutes reflecting on how the whole history of Israel would have been dramatically different if the kings had followed this command. Somehow the kings forgot.

Then everyone had thirty minutes to be alone with the Lord. I asked them to begin by assessing how close they felt to the Lord and to write for a few minutes as they thought about this. They were encouraged to pray and then to copy 1 Peter 5:1-11.

The Lord spoke to *me* as I was copying, but I was not sure that others would sense him speaking to them. We got back together and shared a bit of our experience. I was humbled to hear leader after leader speak of how the Lord had specifically spoken to them. Each one seemed to come away with something different, an insight that directly addressed issues in his or her own spiritual journey. It was obvious that the Holy Spirit had directed and used his Word, his double-edged sword, during our quiet time. It isn't that copying is somehow magic, but it slows us down and allows us more time to let the Word of God penetrate our hearts and judge our thoughts and attitudes (Hebrews 4:12).

Deeply Experiencing the Lord

This winter I began a personal study of Isaiah because I sought to better understand the holiness of God. I already loved several chapters of Isaiah, but frankly there were many more that baffled me.

As I read chapter 1, I decided to copy many of the verses into my
journal. It was so rewarding that I decided to make a condensed copy
of Isaiah in a blank book dedicated exclusively to it. Morning after
morning I was drawn into the Lord's presence as I copied the text. The
love of God touched me in a way it never had before. I could not wait to
get out of bed each morning and begin again. Often I was so moved
that I had no words to express my adoration. I felt strangely silenced—
drinking in God's Word but totally unable to share it. I couldn't even
write what I was experiencing.

Morning after morning, week after week, the sweetness of the
Lord overwhelmed me. And as a byproduct, nature came alive to me
in fresh ways. My eyes were opened to see the beauty of God's holiness. Everywhere I looked there were metaphors of his love. At Carmel, the ocean waves spoke of the ceaseless outpouring of divine
love. Samuel Trevor Francis's hymn "O the Deep, Deep Love of
Jesus" came to mind often:

Oh, the deep, deep love of Jesus,
Vast, unmeasured, boundless, free!
Rolling as a mighty ocean
In its fullness over me.
Underneath me, all around me,
Is the current of his love,
Leading onward, leading homeward
To my glorious rest above.

On campus, leafless elm trees weathering the brunt of winter
spoke of Christ, stripped naked, abandoned, standing silent, alone,
far away from the warmth of the Father's love.

I was tasting the sweetness of the Lord everywhere I went. I had
to find some way to express all that was happening in my soul. Painting, calligraphy and photography became avenues of expressing the

love for which I had no words.

As a result of copying Isaiah, my heart unfolded like little daisy weeds in the campus lawn, opening to bask in the light of the Word. Copying slowed me down, gave me time to contemplate Isaiah's images and metaphors. I understood them. The passages that had always baffled me made sense. I perceived the Lord's beauty, the wonder of his love, the majesty of his holiness as I never have before. It was as if I had *seen* the words before, but now I *perceived* them.

Some months later I picked up an anthology of American literature and happened to read two essays, "A Divine and Supernatural Light" and "Personal Narrative" by Jonathan Edwards. His reflections of his own experience helped me, four hundred years later, to understand mine.

> *Thus there is a difference between having an opinion, that God is holy and gracious, and having a sense of the loveliness and beauty of that holiness and grace. There is a difference between having a rational judgment that honey is sweet, and having a sense of its sweetness. A man may have the former, that knows not how honey tastes; but a man cannot have the latter unless he has an idea of the taste of honey in his mind. So there is the difference between believing that a person is beautiful, and having a sense of his beauty. The former may be obtained by hearsay, but the latter only by seeing the countenance.*[1]

Edwards's words capture how copying Isaiah had allowed my heart to see the beauty of the Lord. Copying has the power to move the words of Scripture from our rational opinions deep into our being. I didn't just know the facts and the stories, I *had tasted*. Now I knew what the psalmist meant: "Taste and see that the LORD is good" (Psalm 34:8).

I encourage you to copy passages of Scripture for yourself, because in copying the text we help ourselves to understand it, to embrace the Lord more deeply.

IN OUR OWN VOICE
Enjoying the Scriptures

His delight is in the law of the Lord.

PSALM 1:2

George Herbert (1593-1633), a rural country pastor, took seriously his own spiritual preparation before he preached or served Communion: he didn't want to be going through the motions but desired to authentically experience the grace of God. Each Sunday morning in the privacy of his personal journal, he wrote poetry. He enjoyed paraphrasing psalms into English poems with regular rhythm and rhyme. He found his paraphrases were easier for his congregation to memorize.

Psalm I

Blest is the man that never would
  in councels of th' ungodly share,

Nor hath in way of sinners stood,
  nor sitten in the scorners chair.

But in God's Law sets his delight,
  and makes that law alone to be
His meditation day and night;
  he shall be like a happy tree,

Which, planted by the waters, shall
  with timely fruit still laden stand:
His leaf shall never fade, and all
  shall prosper that he takes in hand.

The wicked are not so, but they
  are like the chaff, which from the face
Of earth is driven by winds away,
  and finds no sure abiding place.

Therefore shall not the wicked be
  able to stand the Judges doom:
Nor in the safe society
  of good men shall the wicked come.

For God himself vouchsafes to know
  the way that right'ous men have gone:
And those wayes which the wicked go
  shall utterly be overthrown.[1]

Have you ever tried paraphrasing a passage of Scripture? The Living Bible and Eugene Peterson's *The Message* are wonderful, professional examples of putting the Scriptures into everyday speech. It is very challenging work to take familiar passages and rewrite them in modern language, staying true to the author's original intent but expressing it in fresh images and contemporary phrases.

Psalm 1, Living Bible

Oh, the joys of those who do not follow
evil men's advice, who do not hang
around with sinners, scoffing at the things
of God: But they delight in doing everything God wants them to, and day and
night are always meditating on his laws
and thinking about ways to follow him
more closely.

They are like trees along a river bank
luscious fruit each season without fail. Their leaves shall never wither,
and all they do shall prosper.

But for sinners, what a different
story! They blow away like chaff before
the wind. They are not safe on Judgment
Day; they shall not stand among the
godly. For the Lord watches over all
the plans and paths of godly men, but
the paths of the godless lead to doom.

Psalm 1, The Message

How well God must like you—bearing
you don't hang out at Sin Saloon,
you don't slink along Dead-End Road,
you don't go to Smart Mouth College.

Instead you thrill to God's Word,
you chew on Scripture day and night.
You're a tree replanted in Eden,
Bearing fresh fruit every month,
Never dropping a leaf,
always in blossom.

You're not at all like the wicked,
who are mere windblown dust—
Without defense in court,
unfit company for innocent people.

God charts the road you take.
The road they take is Skid Row.

Take on the challenge of paraphrasing a passage of Scripture into
a more contemporary voice. Or try to convert prose into poetry.
Playing with language, even biblical language, can breathe new life
into familiar sections of Scripture.

BRUSHSTROKES
Enjoying a Story

You are the man!
2 SAMUEL 12:7

The Scriptures are full of creative writing: narrative accounts in the Old Testament; poetry, analogies, songs and wordplay in Psalms, Proverbs, Song of Songs, Isaiah. The metaphors, allusions, alliteration and musical qualities are all very creative. Many of the writers make use of extended metaphors—for instance, comparing and contrasting Israel to a vineyard, or God to a wise farmer (Isaiah 5; 28:23-29). With the examples of David and Solomon alone, we should be free to be creative in our journals.

Think about the use of fictitious stories in the Scriptures. The Gospels are full of Jesus' made-up stories, the parables. He created these as he was teaching to make his point. Others used parables as well (for example, Ezekiel 24). Nathan's creative story had quite an impact on David's heart (2 Samuel 12). Ezekiel and other prophets also make use of allegories (Ezekiel 16—17). Some say that the whole book of Song of Songs is an allegory, a story of the love between God and his people. The biblical writers make extensive use of creative writing.

Reflect on Stories

Stories, both true and fictional, often illustrate spiritual truths. Various sources outside of the Scriptures can lead us to spiritual insight. As we write in our journals, it makes sense to consider what we hear and read to see if there is any truth to be gleaned. Often stories we read in the newspaper or watch on television illustrate biblical principles in fresh ways if we take time to reflect on them. For example, I better understood holiness as the natural response to grace as I watched a PBS special titled "The Orphan Trains."*

The Orphan Train ran between 1853 and 1929, as the Children's Aid Society relocated over a hundred thousand orphaned, abandoned or neglected children from the streets of New York City and placed them with families living on farms in the Midwest. Volunteers rounded up these mostly immigrant children in groups of six to 150 for a three-day train ride to farm towns in Ohio or Iowa. The children slept in their seats on the train. They had no idea what the future held for them. The older ones knew it was the luck of the draw—there were no guarantees who would take them home—so they worried.

When the children arrived in a town, people came to the meeting hall to see the homeless children lined up on stage. I was moved by Elliott Hoffman Bobo, now in his eighties, who told his story with tears rolling down his cheeks:

---

*Excerpt quoted with permission from the documentary film "The Orphan Trains" ©1995 Janet Graham and Edward Gray. Available from PBS Video, 800-531 4727 or 877-PBS-SHOP

I *wasn't very comfortable up on that stage because I didn't know where I was going to go. And I was old enough to realize that there could be a lot of mistakes made.*

A farmer came up to me and he felt my muscles and he says, "Oh, you'd make a good hand on the farm." And I says, "Well, I'm not going to go home with you." I says, "You smell too bad. You—you haven't had a bath probably in a year."

And he took me by the arm and was going to lead me off the stage and I bit him. And that didn't work, so I kicked him. And so then everybody in the audience thought I was an incorrigible. They didn't want me because I was out of control.

I was crying there in the chair by myself and a schoolteacher came up there and she says, "I'd like to take you home with me and play with my boy for a week. And if nobody wants you then, why, then we'll have to send you back to New York."

But this elderly couple in their sixties were contacted by this schoolteacher. And they had no children, never did have. They had a stillborn about thirty years previous. So he put me on my—on his lap in this schoolteacher's home and—and got acquainted with me. And he said, "If you go home with me, I'll buy you a pony and a bicycle and a puppy."

So I thought that was great, so I went home with them and I finally got the best home of the whole bunch. But I always thought that biting and kicking did me a lot of good. Best day of my life!

This is the picture—this is the knickers and the high-laced boots and the blouse that I wore on the train. And this is the picture—I first had—I was eight and a half then. I'd been with the—with my parents for six months and they dressed me up for the picture. My mother wanted it when I was all dressed up so she could show it to her relatives. She just wanted to show me off! My father couldn't wait till he could buy my first pony. He just went all over the country trying to find a pony for me. He was a very successful merchant. He owned a hardware store. He was president of the bank. And he owned two farms. I never did work on a farm. He never asked me to.

I never had a spanking. Never had a spanking or any kind of correction.
My dad would put me on his lap and say, "I want you to be a good boy. And
you made some mistakes today and I want you to—to be a good citizen."
And he never did spank me, but I—it got next to me, you know? He wanted
to give me a good start. He—the kindness is what got next to me. He saved
my life. I tried to live the life that Alvin Bobo wanted me to live and I think
I have.

I reflected in my journal on Elliott's story and his remembrance of the kindness of his father:

May I remember the story of the Orphan Train and see the old man with tears running down his cheeks explain how he was alone on the streets of New York until a farmer welcomed him into his home, adopted him and loved him as a son. "His kindness got next to me and I've always tried to live my life to make him proud—and I think I've done that." Yes Lord, I want to live to make you proud, wholly dreading the thought of disappointing, much less rejecting, you.

It was the kindness of the farmer that motivated Elliott to be a good citizen. It is the kindness of God, his undeserved, unearned favor to us, that is to motivate us to repent and live a holy life. A proper understanding of God's grace will lead us "to live our lives to make him proud." It was true for Elliott. It is true for us.

If we watch a television program that moves us or read something that grabs our attention, it makes sense to reflect on the truth in our journals, to let it teach us. Stories have a way of changing our lives.

EXPERIENCE THE BEAUTY
Enjoying Poetry

. . . To praise him for the beauty of his holiness.
2 CHRONICLES 20:21 KJV

For thousands of years poetry has been one of the most loved literary forms. David wrote poetry in spontaneous praise of the Lord.

Praise the LORD.

Praise God in his sanctuary;
  praise him in his mighty heavens.
Praise him for his acts of power;
  praise him for his surpassing greatness.
Praise him with the sounding of the trumpet,
  praise him with the harp and lyre,
praise him with tambourine and dancing
  praise him with the strings and flute,

praise him with the clash of cymbals,
  praise him with resounding cymbals.

Let everything that has breath praise the LORD.
Praise the LORD. (*Psalm 150*)

Give it a try. The poetry you write in your journal may be spontaneous free verse. It may be awful poetry, but who cares? It's the joy of creating it to express your worship or to work out your emotions that counts.

Don't be afraid to try writing poetry. It is a wonderful way of expressing our hearts. I've included some forms in this chapter that you might enjoy trying. Whether or not you generally enjoy reading poetry, you may find writing it helps you to see things in a new way. Try expressing an insight in free verse, or play with one of the many poetic forms.[1] George Herbert's "A Wreath" is a favorite of mine. This poem has a regular rhythm and rhyme pattern. Notice the way he plays with language, twisting the end of each line with the beginning of the next.

A Wreath

A WREATHED *garland of deserved praise,*
Of praise deserved, unto thee I give,
I give to thee, who knowest all my wayes,
My crooked winding wayes, wherein I live,
Wherein I die, not live: for life is straight,
Straight as a line, and ever tends to thee,
To thee, who art more farre above deceit,
Then deceit seems above simplicitie,
Give me simplicitie, that I may live,
So live and like, that I may know, thy wayes,
Know them and practise them: then shall I give
For this poore wreath, give thee a crown of praise.[2]

The poem becomes a wreath; the last line flows back into the first. Herbert mastered playing with words in order to experience the Lord.

Since the sonnet[3] is a traditional form for a love poem, poets have used it to express love for the Lord and the Scriptures, and to contemplate God's love. You may want to take on the challenge. Wrestling your thoughts into poetry of this kind may take several days, or even years. The wrestling is valuable in moving the truth into your soul.

Purpose

These desert angels tend and beasts defend
my lonely vigil. Tempted, taunted, pushed
to prove my might I chased the demon from
my sight. I would not give him power, nor
a chance to take the purpose from my grasp.
With only flesh and bone I fought the war.
My destiny was planned before the world
Took form; before the fruit and worm.
But now I rest with animals close by
and wings surround to comfort. Cup and bread
provided; nourished through the gifts of my
creation. Lowly man won't understand
the reasons for this test, nor fathom why
I'll hang upon a cross, cry out, and die.[4]

You might like to try a villanelle.[5] The form requires that you think a lot about what you want to express. It is fun to try, even if the final results aren't spectacular. Here's one I wrote:

Sustaining Faith

When I feel afraid, remember (a) (first refrain)
Though death is commonplace (b)
The everlasting love of God lasts forever. (second refrain)

Godly people ruined by disaster, (a)
Losses that can never be replaced. (b)
When I feel afraid, remember (first refrain)

Trials come not because I'm a sinner (a)
Fallen far from grace, (b)
The everlasting love of God lasts forever. (second refrain)

So why? godly people, destroy'd, suffer (a)
The falsely accused live with false disgrace (b)
When I feel afraid, remember (first refrain)

The world's not ruled by Lucifer. (a)
He has no sovereignty o'er the human race. (b)
The everlasting love of God lasts forever. (second refrain)

God allows the pain, our purifier (a)
To deepen us as we wait to see his face. (b)
When I feel afraid, remember (first refrain)
The everlasting love of God lasts forever. (second refrain)

Or maybe you'd like to write verse with a chorus, like Psalm 136.

Give thanks to the LORD, for he is good.
  His love endures forever.

Give thanks to the God of gods.
  His love endures forever.
Give thanks to the Lord of lords:
  His love endures forever.
to him who alone does great wonders,
  His love endures forever.

Or write a poem like Psalm 119 expressing your praise for the Scripture. In the original language, every line in the first stanza begins with the first letter of the alphabet, the second stanza with the second letter.

Favorite passages of Scripture or poems can be calligraphed into pictures. Herbert sometimes wrote shaped poems.

The Altar

A BROKEN ALTAR, Lord, thy servant reares,
Made of a heart, and cemented with teares:
Whose parts are as thy hand did frame;
No workman's tool hath touch'd the same.
A HEART alone
Is such a stone,
As nothing but
Thy pow'r doth cut.
Wherefore each part
Of my hard heart
Meets in this frame,
To praise thy Name:
That, if I chance to hold my peace,
These stones to praise thee may not cease.
O let thy blessed SACRIFICE be mine,
And sanctifie this ALTAR to be thine.[6]

There's no limit to the ways in which word art can be integrated into your devotions. Timothy Botts's work is a wonderful example of creating word art with Scripture and verse.

There are lots of forms you can play with—or create your own depending on the image and meaning of the poem (as Herbert did with "A Wreath"). When you feel inspired this week, try to write some poetry. Our own poetry, and the poetry of others, written in our journals can enhance our worship times.[7]

21

BEYOND WORDS
Enjoying Artistic Touches

Set up some large stones and coat them with plaster.
Write on them all the words of this law. . . . You shall write very clearly
all the words of this law on these stones you have set up.
DEUTERONOMY 27:2-3, 8

Journals need not be limited to words alone. Feel free to bring drawing or painting into your devotional time. Maybe you'd like to use calligraphy, or draw a border, or use various colors of pens or crayons.

One day I wanted to think about what Jackie did that made me feel so welcomed when I went to her home. So I created a border around a page in my journal, "Welcome Welcome Welcome," with my calligraphy pen. As I was doing that, I thought about the specific ways Jackie had welcomed me. When I had finished the border, I wrote my thoughts.

Welcome. Welcome. Welcome. Welcome. Welcome. Welcome. Welcome.

Jackie's eyes sparkle and look deeply into mine. "It's so good to see you." She looks into my eyes, pouring into my soul her love. Her hug lasts a moment longer than others. Her attention stays focused . . . stays focused . . . stays with me just a little while longer than it needed to. "I'm so glad you could come." Her eyes still sparkle with love, her warm love that welcomes me into her home, into her friendship, into her love.

I've seen Jackie welcome all of us this way, as if no one else was in the room. It's a gift of her presence she gives us. She intentionally makes sure that we know we are welcome. We can relax. We believe her. It was good that we came.

Lord, help me to truly welcome others as Jackie does and as you will one day welcome me. You said, "I am going to my Father's house to prepare a place for you. And if I go and prepare a place for you, I will come back and take you to be with me that you also may be where I am." How incredible.

Welcome. Welcome. Welcome. Welcome. Welcome. Welcome. Welcome.

Sometimes when I'm studying a passage, I get out color crayons and draw it. Once I asked an adult Sunday school class to draw Revelation 4 after we had read it together. Stick figures were fine. When we had finished drawing, we talked about what we drew.

A week later as we were beginning class, I asked the group how many elders surround the Lord's throne. What do they do? What do they say? What does it look like? Everyone could answer. They had drawn twenty-four thrones and they remembered. They had drawn the colors of the rainbow and the crystal river, so they remembered. They hadn't been studying the passage during the week—there's just something about drawing that embeds an image in our minds.

Some passages of Old Testament prophecy come to life in new ways when you get out your crayons. It might also be helpful to draw pictures to summarize a book of the Bible you've been studying, or as an overview of a talk you plan to give. If you are at all visual, the images and colors will stick in your memory a long time.

Images for Our Lives

Coloring before beginning to write gets our thoughts flowing. We discover things that we didn't know before we began. Sue Monk Kidd, a longtime editor of *Guideposts*, describes this experience of sketching a scene only to realize it represented her inner struggle:

> I sighed, my mind wandering to the picture I'd sketched the night before. (I have a hobby of charcoal drawing, and lately I'd found solace in my sketchpad.) The previous evening I'd drawn a tent in the middle of some windhowling woods. The stakes that secured the bottom of the tent were uprooted, and the flaps were flailing in the wind. As I put down my pencil, I said to myself, "That's my life." Indeed, it seemed as if the stakes that had secured my neat, safe existence—stakes that I had spent most of my life carefully nailing down—had been pulled up, and everything was tossing about. Underneath the sketch, I wrote, "Midlife."[1]

At spiritual renewal retreats I've asked women to color pictures that represent their spiritual journey. It is frightening to be asked to draw a picture. Just about everyone panics. But risk is good—it develops our faith—so we draw. It leads us to remember how the Lord met us in specific instances as children, in high school, during college and in adulthood. Some of us write out favorite verses. Some create a design. Some have a very specific memory that they draw. Some draw a tree, or a desk, or forty-one baby carriages—images that are symbolic (forty-one foster babies!) of the Lord's presence in life's journey. Then we write for twenty minutes about what we've drawn—what the images mean.

Throughout our three days together, each has the opportunity to share her drawing. It is incredible how the Lord uses drawing to bring out very significant images. Over and over again the women marvel at how significant this drawing exercise was for them.

Try spending thirty minutes drawing how the Lord has met you, drawing a place, or an image, or a specific experience, or the crucifixion, and see what you discover.

Along with drawing, I love to take pictures of scenes that speak to me of the Lord. On my desk I have a photograph of a path through the woods near where I grew up. It reminds me of the Lord's invitation to come walk with him. I have a photo of a Civil War cemetery in my journal. It speaks to me of the soldier's sacrifice from 2 Timothy 2. Many times the Lord commanded the children of Israel to create a visual reminder (Numbers 17:1-11; Deuteronomy 27:1-8; Joshua 4:1-24; 8:32).

Have you ever chosen a visual image, a metaphor, of what you want to become? Living metaphors can help us picture the character qualities we seek to develop. An old elm tree on campus has become my tree. It speaks to me of spiritual things as it changes throughout the seasons. This spring my tree had literally millions of seeds that were blown by the wind all over that part of the campus. What a picture of spreading the gospel this was for me. Bringing such images home as drawings or photographs helps me to continue to reflect on what they can teach me.

An altar of stones taken from the Jordan river, covered in plaster and inscribed with the words of Moses, was an ordained, visual reminder to Israel of the faithfulness of God. In our journals we can create pictures—windows into our inner struggles, testimonies of God's hand in our life, metaphors of the character traits that we hope to develop. Feel free going beyond words in your journal.

INSIGHT
Writing to Learn from an Author

*And the things you have heard me say in the
presence of many witnesses entrust to reliable men
who will also be qualified to teach others.*

2 TIMOTHY 2:2

Writing in my journal as I read a book often substantially expands my understanding. As I take an author's insight and reflect on it for a while, I am able to integrate her ideas into my own thinking. I come to understand them. This is true for secular books as well as for Christian books. (It is also true for the Bible, although this chapter focuses on other books.) Often as I'm writing, the author's insight leads me into new insight of my own.

There are so many great books to read. Books that were written this year. Books from several hundred years ago. I usually have several books going at the same time. If I lose interest in a book, I don't feel compelled to finish it. Sometimes I read books that push the borders of my comfort zone—ones that really challenge my thinking, ones I disagree with.

Often I ask people what they are reading, and in my journal I keep a list of books I want to read. I never get to read all of them, but I do get to read some. At least the list is a starting point when I'm searching for a good book. Henri Nouwen encourages us to regularly read good books:

> Do we really want our minds to become the garbage can of the world? Clearly we do not, but it requires real discipline to let God and not the world be the Lord of our mind. But that asks of us not just to be gentle as doves, but also cunning as serpents! Therefore spiritual reading is such a helpful discipline. Is there a book we are presently reading, a book that we have selected because it nurtures our mind and brings us closer to God? . . . Even if we were to read for only fifteen minutes a day in such a book, we would soon find our mind becoming less of a garbage can and more of a vase filled with good thoughts.[1]

I enjoy reading good books that fill me with insight. Sometimes these books have nothing overtly to do with Christian life or the church, yet as I read, I see principles that speak to me spiritually. I also love to read the writings of someone who has lived a long while with the Lord and can lead me to better understand him.

Many authors have become my spiritual mentors. As Jonathan Edwards helped me to understand what I was learning about spending time in silence with the Lord, others have helped me to understand other aspects of my life. Sometimes I ask myself questions based on their words, as if they were questioning me. Sometimes I reflect on how their insight informs my perspective. As I read, I pause to write.

Learning from Secular Authors

Truth comes to us from many places. A book doesn't need to be a Christian book to teach us. In Shelley Harwayne's *Lasting Impres-*

sions[2] a warning to public school teachers, "Beware of the cute idea," struck me. Teacher curriculum is full of cute ideas that sometimes have little to do with real learning. As a Sunday school teacher, I needed to think about this. *Am I depending on cute ideas provided in the curriculum instead of on authentic responses to the Scripture as the basis for my lessons?* Harwayne wasn't writing about Sunday school, but I applied her insight to my situation. I decided to rethink my goals for Sunday school and how I could best lead my class there:

"Beware of the cute idea!"

Authenticity is the filter. Does this work in my life? I never want to pass on to others, to teach what seems good as it's described in the Sunday school material if it has not worked for me. In order to pass on my love and devotion for Christ, I need to share the stories, my own and others, the stories that have shaped me. The Scripture isn't dead. It's alive—the real stories of real people who had their lives changed. Getting the students to meet these people and walk in their shoes for a while and experience what they did will be key. Beware of the cute idea.

Harwayne's beautiful writing also prompted a question that led to unexpected places.

What is it about good writing—fiction or non-fiction—that seems to open me to spiritual things? I think it has to do with "the story." You don't analyze, just enjoy, it slips past the defenses and lands in your heart—it allows you to ponder, question, view the thought from different vantage points with no conclusions. With stories, I draw the conclusion. I determine what it means and I'm open to my maxim—they're not judgmental and I don't have to be defensive—I can allow the story in and in coming in, it may change my whole way of looking at the world. Once my paradigm shifts—behavior soon follows. Interesting to think of how Moses wanted the people of Israel to recount their story annually so they wouldn't forget. David was up to his ears in sin and totally in denial. Nathan made up a story and David's heart was pierced. Jesus chose parables to teach principles so that those who had ears to hear—would be able to hear. And then those with stubborn hearts wouldn't be hardened any further. We never tire of hearing stories. Tell me an old, old story.

Why have we given up the well-told story and replaced it with an outline and three points and cute ideas?

This pondering changed how I teach children and adults. While some think that stories should not be used in "real" Bible teaching, I'm convinced that they play a huge role in touching hearts and changing lives. And my conviction about the importance of stories was crystallized as I pondered my response to a book for elementary public school teachers.

Learning from Godly Authors

Recently I read a Henri Nouwen passage[3] about how our lives are gifts we are supposed to share. It was a new way to think about my life. I reflected on it in my journal, holding it in my hand, rotating the idea so that I could see it from various angles:

"My life is a gift to be shared." In the center of myself, I am not something I can conquer. (Conquer my diet. Conquer my bad habits.) I am what has been given to me. I am worth more than the result of all my efforts. Being is more important than having or doing. My life is not a possession to be defended, but a gift to be shared. The words I speak are not just my own, but are given to me. The love I have is not my love, but a love that has been given to me; it too is a gift to me—a gift for me to share. All I am, all of my wisdom, all of my love, all of my joy, all of my pain, all of the spirituality or lack of it, all of my education and ability to learn—all of it is a gift

to me from the Lord. But it is not a gift for me to cling to, to hide under the bed, and to possess. These gifts are not a box of Frango mints! The Father has given me these gifts including my humanity with its shortcomings, and this life is a gift he intended for me to share. Father, teach me how to live in such a way that my life is a gift I share. All of it—the good, the struggle, the pain.

When we are required to read a book or article in school, often we are asked to write a page of response to the author's ideas. This writing usually includes a summary of the text along with our own thoughts. During my graduate work, I wrote several hundred pages responding to what I was reading. After two years of doing this in my coursework, I wrote my thesis. On several occasions I was shocked by how close I came to quoting without realizing it. It became obvious that in the process of reading and then writing about the ideas of others, I had fully integrated their thoughts into my own thinking. Their thoughts were now my thoughts.

Now I regularly write a page of response to what I'm reading, either in my journal or at the end of the chapter in the book. Even though I am no longer in school and no one is requiring that I write responsively, I still do. Otherwise the insights slip away rather quickly. I need to *use* the new thoughts if I want them to become mine. I don't always feel like writing a page of response, but I know the discipline will pay off in establishing the new truth firmly in my thinking. Use your journal to learn from others, so that their thinking can inform and become your own.

INTEGRATION
Writing to Think and Synthesize

Hold on to instruction, do not let it go;
guard it well, for it is your life.
PROVERBS 4:13

Often we are asked to write to express on paper what we already know. When we complete this kind of an assignment, our thinking will be sharpened. Writing is one of the most powerful tools for thinking. In fact, some teachers go so far as to say that writing is the key to learning.[1] As we write, beginning with what we know, we can think our way to a new, deeper level of understanding.[2]

William Zinsser explains:

> *Writing organizes and clarifies our thoughts. Writing is how we think our way into a subject and make it our own. Writing enables us to find out what we know—and what we don't know—about whatever we're trying to learn. Putting an idea into written words is like defrosting the windshield:*

The idea, so vague out there in the murk, slowly begins to gather itself into a sensible shape. Whatever we write—a memo, a letter, a note to the baby-sitter—all of us know this moment of finding out what we really want to say by trying in writing to say it.[3]

This learning aspect of writing can be employed in journaling to help us develop a deeper understanding of our faith (one of many possible topics) and prepare us to be salt and light in the world (Matthew 5:13-14).

Learning to Tell the Story

Perhaps we want to share our testimony of how we came to know Christ but we are not sure where to begin. Everyone at church probably assumes that we know what to say, but we don't. The fact that we came to faith doesn't mean that we know how to lead someone else to faith. So we are uncomfortable at the thought of talking to nonbelievers about Jesus. We hesitate to share the good news because we aren't confident we will say it right.

This is a perfect opportunity to use our journal. By writing out our story of coming to faith, we will learn. Writing to learn what we know (our experience) can serve as the basis for learning what we don't know. As we write, we learn.

What is your testimony? How did you come to know your need for Christ? When did you make a decision to trust him as your Savior? You may want to write your story in your journal. Working to write your testimony in three to four pages may help you to think it through so that you feel comfortable sharing it with someone else.

Go back and integrate the fundamental truths of the gospel into your story. How did you come to know that God loves you? When did you realize you were a sinner? Why does it make sense that all sin deserves punishment? How can Jesus' death be the payment for sin? What were you thinking as you decided to put your trust in Jesus? What Bible passages do you know that support each of these aspects of the gospel message? What illustrations might help your friends to understand these ideas? Writing to answer these questions will help us to learn the gospel, and to share the gospel with others in our own authentic voice. We write to learn.

What Does It Mean to Hear?

This year I've been writing to understand what it means to "hear God." It concerns me that many American Christians casually use the phrase "God told me." Does God tell us to marry a certain person by giving us specific revelation of his will? Through Scripture or through our thoughts as we pray, does God tell us to enter into a major business venture? Many believe that God "confirms with Scripture" a decision they are considering. They then take this confirmation to mean that God *called* them to a specific position of service. Is this biblical? I have been writing in my journal to explore what it means to "hear" God.

I wasn't really concerned about how God was speaking to other people. I felt it was time to clarify my belief about how God would speak to *me*. Should I seek some kind of mystical confirmation as I read Scripture before I accept a position to serve in the church? Quite honestly, I resist the notion of hearing God, because I never know when a thought is God's word to me or my own crazy idea.

I spent some time journaling about what I thought it means when people say, "God told me . . ." I reflected on what I thought hearing God might mean and what I thought it cannot mean. I reflected on times when I thought I heard God and considered whether I really had. I also talked with various people and reflected in my journal on what they said. I set aside several pages to chronicle my insights into "hearing God."

I also read various Scripture passages and wrote about how people in the Old Testament (Eve, Abraham, Moses, the boy Samuel, David) heard God. I looked for principles from their experience that I thought might apply to me today. I looked at passages in the New Testament. I found Luke's account of the parable of the sower very insightful (Luke 8:4-15).

In *The Soul at Rest* Tricia Rhodes leads readers through a Bible study on listening to God. After I finished the study, I wrote in my journal what I concluded from that study, where I agreed and disagreed with the conclusions Rhodes was leading to.

In my writing, I reflected on times when people in work or ministry teams with me had been very sure they had heard God. It seemed to me that sometimes when this happened, the group stopped thinking. Once someone said "The Lord told me . . ." the group became passive. The members thought that we were not in a position to say God had *not* spoken, so instead of reasoning to a conclusion, we chose to do what "God had said." The group reasoned, *If God said it and we didn't do it, wouldn't that be disobedience? Wouldn't that be sin?* In my journal I felt free to look back on times this happened and wonder if we should have responded differently.

Then I began Dallas Willard's *Hearing God* and wrestled with his thoughts on the topic. As he establishes initial guidelines regarding what it means to hear God, he says:

> This brings us to the third preliminary truth that we must keep constantly before us in our search for a word from God: When God speaks to us, it does not prove that we are righteous or even right. It does not even prove that we have correctly understood what he said. The infallibility of the messenger and the message does not guarantee the infallibility of our reception. Humility is always in order.
>
> This is an especially important point to make since the appeals "God told

me" or "the Lord led me" are commonly used by the speaker to prove that "I
am right," that "you should follow me" or even that "I should get my way."
Once for all let us say that no such claim is automatically justified.[4]

Willard had my attention. He was addressing my questions. I
continued reading eagerly. I wrote in the margins throughout the
book to help me understand his points. Often at the end of a chapter
I tried to put my thinking into words. When I completed the book I
typed up my notes. I tried to summarize his thoughts and I also
incorporated my responses. I wrote questions about what I didn't
understand.

As I wrote to learn I integrated all of my study with my own experiences. By the end of my study, I had fourteen pages of single-spaced
writing to summarize my current understanding about what it means
and does not mean to hear God. From launching the study until the
end, my thinking had broadened substantially.

Using a journal to write our way to a deeper understanding of
any topic is one of the best ways, if not *the* best way, to learn. We are
"making what we are learning our own, making meaning for ourselves. We make links between what we already know and are trying
to learn."[5] This meaning-making happens as we write.

24

APPROACH
Writing to Invite the Word of God In

In the beginning was the Word . . . and the Word was God.
JOHN 1:1

The previous two chapters discussed how to use writing to learn from any written text: secular, Christian or biblical. Before looking at additional ways to use journal writing as we read, we need to consider ourselves as readers. Are we coming to the text as a learner? This is a formational question. *How we approach a text will affect the extent to which it can change us.*

There are many ways to approach a book. Sometimes we skim pages quickly, looking for a main idea. Sometimes we read and reread a paragraph, trying to comprehend the author's meaning. Our purpose for reading determines how carefully we engage the text.

When we read the Bible and want to pay close attention, we can use our journal to keep a log of our thinking. Mortimer Adler suggests that we can tell if we are doing a good job of reading if we have something written to show for it:

> Not only should [reading] tire you, but there should be some discernible product of your mental activity. Thinking usually tends to express itself overtly in language. One tends to verbalize ideas, questions, difficulties, judgments that occur in the course of thinking. If you have been reading, you must have been thinking; you have something you can express in words. One of the reasons why I find reading a slow process is that I keep a record of the little thinking I do. I cannot go on reading the next page, if I do not make a memo of something which occurred to me in reading this one.[1]

What do we think about while we read? Teachers and theorists have for the past century debated this question and have discussed two stances, two approaches that are at opposite ends of a spectrum. Readers assume a *stance* as they come to a text. How you approach a text, I believe, will shape what you think as you read.

Accumulating Facts, Experiencing the Text

At one end of the spectrum is the reader on a quest for facts and bits of information to take home. This kind of reader is like the six-year-old who interrupts as you begin your Sunday school lesson to say that he already knows this story. What he means is that he already knows the facts. He knows that "Zacchaeus was a short tax collector who climbed a tree to see Jesus, and Jesus went to have dinner with Zacchaeus, and afterwards Zacchaeus gave back all of the money he had stolen" (from Luke 19). This little boy has a pretty good idea of the facts—the *who? what? when? where?*—so he doesn't understand what more he will gain from your telling him the story again. Louise Rosenblatt, professor emerita of English education at New York University, calls this stance "efferent" (from the Latin *effere*, to carry away).[2] If you are reading for facts, what you think about and then what you write in your journal would be the information, factual observations you make as you are reading. That's what you'd carry away. But isn't there more to Bible reading than carrying home a pocketful of facts?

At the opposite end of the spectrum is the reader who comes to the text to experience it, to be fully absorbed in rich language and images and the responses evoked as she is reading. Rosenblatt terms this an "aesthetic" stance—it is the experience of going to a five-star restaurant and enjoying the tastes, the perfectly seasoned carrot ginger soup, the smoked salmon and capers, the presentation of the asparagus, drizzled and garnished. We could read the chef's recipe cards and take away lots of information about what we were served, but that really would not capture the essence. If you are reading to experience, then typically what you think about as you read is your response, your *Aha!* discoveries, your anger, your ponderings. Your journal would contain a response log.

Reading doesn't have to be only for information or just for experience. That's Rosenblatt's point. How we read a text is our choice. Rosenblatt believes that readers can move back and forth, seeking information that evokes a response that sends them back to the text for more information. Unfortunately, in my opinion, we are not taught to read aesthetically. So we may not be aware of our feelings and thoughts as we read. And sadly, we may have been taught that the only *appropriate* way to read the Bible is efferently, to gather the facts and the main idea.

Let's come to the Scriptures to gather the facts *and* to experience the truth, "to let the truth settle from our heads down into our hearts."[3] Writing in a journal can help us become aware of what we are thinking and how we are approaching a text. Are we coming to get information? Are we coming to experience the text? I hope we are coming for both. The bottom-line question is, *am I experiencing the truth?*

Theologian M. Robert Mulholland Jr. underlines the importance of the stance we take as we come to the Scriptures. We can come for the purpose of mastering the text and become very adept at keeping it at arm's length. It seems to me that this is precisely what the Pharisees during Jesus' time were doing. We need to ask, Am I *resisting letting the Scriptures confront me? Am I coming only to be informed?* Mulholland explains:

> We have a deeply ingrained way of reading in which we are the masters of the material we read. We come to a text with our own agenda firmly in place, perhaps not always consciously but usually subconsciously. . . . The rational, cognitive, intellectual dynamics of our being go into full operation to analyze, critique, dissect, reorganize, synthesize, and digest the material we find appropriate to our agenda. . . . We control our approach to the text; we control our interaction with the text; we control the impact of the text upon our lives.[4]

It's not that reading for information or mastery of the text is wrong. Certainly we must know the facts. But let's not stop there. We can become readers who move back and forth between gathering information and opening our hearts to an encounter with the living God. Becoming aware of our heart's response while we are fact-gathering allows both our heart and our mind to be engaged as we read. We can come to be transformed.

Reading and Writing for Transformation

Writing in our journal as we read allows us to take the information and ask ourselves hard questions for the purpose of being "rebuked, corrected and trained in righteousness" (see 2 Timothy 3:16). As we befriend the biblical characters and carefully consider what life was like for them, their lives can challenge us. We can learn from their mistakes and be encouraged by their faith.

Since we believe that there is more to the Bible than its facts and that the Word of God is living and active (Hebrews 4:12), used by the Holy Spirit to lay bare the thoughts and attitudes of our hearts, our journal writing as we read the Word can reflect our *need*. Writing as we read the Bible helps us assume a posture of listening and learning, laid bare before the Holy Spirit—defenses down. Our writing is then an integral part of our transformation.

As we begin to write our responses to the Bible, it makes sense to acknowledge that we come with our history. We bring our life experiences with us. If we write our thoughts as we read, we can intentionally open all of our life, bringing out of the hidden places our reactions, emotions, past sins, fears. Being aware of our experience and our thoughts as we read brings various pieces of our life together with the insight of others and the truths of Scripture to change us into Christ's likeness.

What is your approach to the Bible? Do you keep a safe distance? Do you keep your defensive shield in place? If we choose, we can use our journal to open ourselves to encounter the Word of God, who breaks into our world and comes near.

> I *saw heaven standing open and there before me was a white horse, whose rider is called Faithful and True. With justice he judges and makes war. His eyes are like blazing fire, and on his head are many crowns. He has a name written on him that no one knows but he himself. He is dressed in a robe dipped in blood, and his name is the Word of God.* (Revelation 19:11-13)

As you approach the text of Scripture, be aware that you are coming to encounter the risen Christ, the Word of God.

REFLECTION
Writing to Walk into the Scriptures

Reflect on what I am saying,
for the Lord will give you insight into all this.
2 TIMOTHY 2:7

Studying Scripture requires focused, sustained thought. Journaling during Scripture study helps us to think, to walk into the text and have it expand into a whole new world.

As we saw in the previous chapter, studying the Bible can become an academic endeavor, involving the mind without ever penetrating the heart. If the Word of God is to really penetrate our thinking so that it transforms us, it is important that we approach the text with an openness to the Holy Spirit's work in us.

We write in our journal as we approach, to assess our stance as we come to the text. We also write to ruminate on the truths we encounter. Writing gives us time to think deeply about an idea, seeing it from many vantage points while it settles into our heart.

When I take time to stay awhile in one verse, I see more. I walk into the text through questions, writing what puzzles or confuses me. My questions lead me further into the passage. I feel like Lucy as she explores the enormous wardrobe for the first time and finds herself in Narnia.

> *"This must be a simply enormous wardrobe!" thought Lucy, going still further in and pushing the soft folds of the coats aside to make room for her. Then she noticed that there was something crunching under her feet. "I wonder is that more moth-balls?" she thought, stooping down to feel it with her hands. But instead of feeling the hard, smooth wood of the floor of the wardrobe, she felt something soft and powdery and extremely cold. "This is very queer," she said, and went on a step or two further.*[1]

Reflecting on a biblical text often opens up whole new worlds of insight.

How do we reflect on a text? I try to see the connections within it: how does this paragraph relate to the previous paragraph and to the one before that one? I speculate on the purpose of the paragraph and work to understand it in light of the whole book. *If this is true, then what does that mean about other passages of Scripture?* I weave in my stories and my past experiences, pose questions, seek information, wonder about possibilities, talk with other people, draw conclusions, visualize what it means when it is lived out in life, make inferences, peek around corners.

Sustained Thought

As I was reading Colossians, I came across the verse that said we are to be "devoted to prayer." So I paused to reflect on the word *devoted*.

 What does this mean, "be devoted to prayer"? Should our conversation with the Lord, our sense of living in his presence be foremost in

*our thoughts? I'd say we should be totally given to prayer if it is to be our
"devotion."*

How interesting to think of being devoted—it means totally in love and
given to something. We call our quiet times "our devotions." Devotion—a
very common word, but what does it mean? Persist and continue in—seems
that my devotions have very little to do with feeling devotion towards the
Lord.

Col. 4:2 Devote yourselves to prayer, being watchful and thankful.

In English, "to be devoted" incorporates the idea of eagerness: intense,
abandoned, passionate, on fire, dedicated, committed. Am I devoted to
prayer? Planning to pray relentlessly until God acts?

If we are going to be devoted to something it takes all our interest, our pri-
mary focus. People devoted to quilting are obsessed with quilting. They talk
about quilts, have quilts all over their homes. They quilt during every spare
minute. Am I devoted to prayer?

Writing helps me to sustain focused thought for a long period of
time so that I can figure out what I think. Often as I conclude my
devotional time I write a prayer, typically a request that the Lord
will bring about the necessary change.

Often reflecting on a text bears fruit over time. It sits on the back
burner and simmers until it finally all comes together. It's not just as
I sit at my desk that I reflect on a passage. I think about it all day
long. Because I'm writing today and know that I will be writing
again tomorrow (or sometime soon), my mind wrestles with ideas
when I don't even know it. As I'm folding laundry or riding my bike
or fixing dinner I'm struck with a new idea about a topic I'm pondering. It's exciting when this happens. I can't wait to get my journal
so I can write it down. As long as I'm looking for answers, my mind
keeps working, percolating, seeking.

In my study of 1 and 2 Timothy, I had been getting to know Timothy and the people in the church he pastored. Our ministry was being criticized—*we* were being criticized—and I wanted to learn from Timothy how to respond. One Saturday I spent an hour on a plane working my way through 2 Timothy, writing down all of the principles of ministry that Paul gives to Timothy. I noticed that many of the principles were falling into categories—prayer, mentoring, encouragement. Then I noticed the three analogies Paul gives Timothy: the soldier, the athlete, the farmer:

> *Endure hardship with us like a good soldier of Christ Jesus. No one serving as a soldier gets involved in civilian affairs—he wants to please his commanding officer. Similarly, if anyone competes as an athlete, he does not receive the victor's crown unless he competes according to the rules. The hardworking farmer should be the first to receive a share of the crops. Reflect on what I am saying, for the Lord will give you insight into all this.* (2 Timothy 2:3-7)

What did Paul hope Timothy would learn from these comparisons? I brainstormed a list beginning with the question, *How is Christian leadership like being a solider?* I wrote down every possible connection I could think of. Then the plane landed and I walked into a busy day of meetings. Sunday I was back home, spending the day in church activities.

The following Monday, when my husband and I went for a bike ride, all kinds of ideas were popping to mind about what we can learn from the soldier, the athlete and the farmer. Apparently without any conscious thought I had been considering all of this while I was doing other things. When we returned from the ride, I wrote in my journal:

> *A soldier wears a uniform, eats rations, lives in a tent, leaves his family behind. He focuses only on the objective. He's under orders. He is submitted: "Sir, yes sir." He makes the highest sacrifice. He is expend-*

able for the higher cause. He's in danger. He's at risk. There's a sense in which a solider doesn't evaluate, question, rationalize, or give his opinions. He executes commands. The soldier doesn't see the bigger picture, he simply follows orders. The soldier does his part and trusts that the commanding officer has the whole campaign in mind. Each solider is expendable. He cannot save the world, but he can accomplish his piece of the objective.

It's easy to read quickly through 2 Timothy 2:3-7 and never spend time reflecting on what Paul is saying. It is as we ask questions and pause to ponder a phrase that it can really challenge us. As I continued to reflect on the comparison of Christian service to military service, I came to realize that my sole focus is to be on pleasing the Lord. I don't need to worry about disgruntled people. I need to focus on pleasing my commanding officer. I also learned that I don't need to understand everything that happens to me. *I'm expendable,* and I trust that the Lord has the bigger picture in mind as he sends me into battle. I shouldn't be shocked by the fact that I am at risk. All who seriously intend to follow Jesus will be at risk. ("In fact, everyone who wants to live a godly life in Christ Jesus will be persecuted," 2 Timothy 3:12.)

Is there a question you are pondering? Have you seen a metaphor you would like to think more about? Take time to write about them in your journal. Write down your thinking as you spend time reflecting on metaphors, brainstorming possibilities and pondering what the Scriptures mean in light of your current experiences. You may get to a point where you don't have anything left to write. You may need to simply meditate on the passage in the Lord's presence.

From Reflecting to Meditating

Many people move from reading the Bible, to meditating on the Scriptures, to withdrawing into a period of silence to prayerfully focus on the text.[2] Meditation is an ancient practice. The Lord commanded Joshua to meditate: "Do not let this Book of the Law depart from your mouth; meditate on it day and night, so that you may be careful to do everything written in it" (Joshua 1:8). There is a time to put our pen down and stop writing in our journal. By sitting in silence we position ourselves to hear God's word *to us*, allowing the meaning to emerge and transform us in the deep places of our heart, mind and soul. We ask God to speak his word into our being and we sit in silence, simply *being* in his presence, focused on the text of Scripture we've selected.

Stay awhile. The first time I did this, it felt like an eternity to sit silently for fifteen minutes. I couldn't figure out what I was supposed to get out of it. But with practice, silence and meditation have become a precious aspect of my worship. Reflection and meditation draw us through the Bible into the presence of God.

DIALOGUE JOURNALING
Writing to Respond to God's Word

Do your best to present yourself to God as one . . .
who correctly handles the word of truth.

2 TIMOTHY 2:15

I use my journal to help me know Jesus—to better understand and respond to him and to the Scriptures. Dialogue journaling through narrative accounts helps me to hear the Word of God, see the biblical characters in action, listen to the conversations, wonder how I would have reacted, experience the scene *as if* I *were there.* As a result, I better understand the Scriptures and myself.

Pastor C. H. Spurgeon (1834-1892) preached to a congregation of over six thousand in London. He exhorts us not to simply quote John 3:16 and think we know the love of God. We need to go to the cross to see the Savior's love: "The common mercies we enjoy all sing of love, just as the sea-shell, when we put it to our ears, whispers of the deep sea whence it came; but if we desire to hear the ocean itself, we must not look at everyday blessings, but at the transactions of the crucifixion. He who would know love, *let him retire to Calvary* and see the Man of sorrows die."[1] Spurgeon obviously spent time experiencing the accounts of Christ's passion. His *Morning and Evening Daily Readings* are full of the personal insight he received as he mentally went to the cross and experienced the Savior's love. By writing a dialogue, putting into words a conversation with the text, we too can go to Calvary and see Jesus.

Not long ago I was asked to share some thoughts on what it means to live by faith. As I prepared, I decided to probe the Scriptures to consider what it meant for John the Baptist to live by faith. It actually took me three months and twenty-five pages to dialogue journal through the narrative accounts of John's life and death. It is one of my favorite studies. The first page appears below so you can see what dialogue journaling looks like for me.

I began with one passage which led me to related passages as I sought to understand the facts, as well as the sights and sounds, the attitudes and implications, the joy and the despair of John the Baptist's life and ministry. The first passage was Matthew 3:1-7. As I read verse 8, I began to write. These are the words I wrote. The Scripture verses that I copied into my journal are followed by my responses. The journal entry is a written dialogue between me and the text. Asking questions as I read—hard questions that don't have easy answers, honest questions that I want to know the answers to—forms the gateway into the text.

Confessing their sins, they were baptized by him in the Jordan River. But when he [John] saw many of the Pharisees and Sadducees coming to where he was baptizing, he said to them: "You brood of vipers! Who warned you to flee from the coming wrath?" (Matthew 3:6-7)

What kind of a question is this? John was warning everyone. Did John hate these people to the point that he wanted them to feel the heat of the wrath of God? He certainly didn't nicely win them over to Jesus. He hit them head on, invective, name-calling: "brood of vipers." He almost sounds mad that they would come out to see what was going on. No baptism for the self-righteous but a baptism for repentance, not for those who think they are healthy but for the sick.

> Produce fruit in keeping with repentance. And do not think you can say to yourselves, "We have Abraham as our father." I tell you that out of these stones God can raise up children for Abraham. (Matthew 3:8)

Quite a speech to the Pharisees, "Bring forth fruit." What weren't they doing? They weren't walking by faith and trusting in God. They were trusting in their lineage to Abraham and their good works. John wants them to produce fruit in keeping with repentance. (Well what kind of fruit?) Didn't the Pharisees have all of the fruit, the rules about how to keep the Law? Weren't they disciplined to the max? So what did John want them to produce? What change was he demanding? They certainly must have gotten the picture that adding his baptism to the status quo wouldn't cut it (Luke 11:33).

> "Isaiah was right when he prophesied about you hypocrites; as it is written: 'These people honor me with their lips, but their hearts are far from me. They worship me in vain; their teachings are but rules taught by men.' You have let go of the commands of God and are holding on to the traditions of men." And he said to them: "You have a fine way of setting aside the commands of God in order to observe your own traditions!" (Mark 7:1-23)

> Then Jesus came from Galilee to the Jordan to be baptized by John. But John tried to deter him, saying, "I need to be baptized by you, and do you come to me?" (Matthew 3:13)

Are there times when we know something is inappropriate, not our place, reserved for someone else not us, and we walk by faith when Jesus says Yes, this is to fulfill all righteousness. "How can this be?" John must have thought but he went along with it. "OK. I'll trust you." There have been times when I felt something wasn't my place. I think, "Lord, I don't know . . . but I'll trust."

In journaling with Scripture we slow down enough to see what's there and pray that the Lord will work his truth into our lives. We write out parts of the Scripture that we want to think about and ask questions of ourselves from the text as they come to mind.

As we write these thoughts down, we may find we are praying, bringing together our response to the text and our daily experiences in Jesus' presence. We try to figure out what it means for how we should live our lives.

Often I will then begin to write out a prayer to the Lord about what this Scripture means in my life. But this is generally unintentional. My writing begins to unconsciously move from a rambling of loosely connected questions and thoughts in response to the Scripture to a focused prayer. It shifts from a dialogue of my response to the Word to a dialogue with Jesus and my response to him. By the end, I'm addressing the Lord more than myself. It's a gradual, invisible, unconscious process. I have repeatedly seen this pattern: I begin with a text, and as I ponder it, my audience shifts. I'm no longer figuring something out, I'm praying. Usually I wouldn't even think of this journaling as a prayer, except that I naturally conclude with Amen.

Use your journal to write your way into a full understanding of Scripture, whether you focus on a short phrase or on a hard question. Actively, persistently and carefully consider what it says; ruminate over time on what it means. If it's a narrative account, imagine that you were there, experience what the people in the story experienced, stay awhile with them, learning. Be aware of your thoughts as you read, and record your questions and your reactions. Go to cross-references and commentaries or other reference works to find answers to your questions. Seek to experience the truth. Open the door of your heart and invite the Holy Spirit in to transform you to be more like Christ.

Part 3

VENTURING OUT

Go now, write it on a tablet for them,
inscribe it on a scroll,
that for the days to come
it may be an everlasting witness.
ISAIAH 30:8

27

ATTIC GOLD
The Art of Letter Writing

Paul, an apostle . . . to Timothy, my dear son.
2 TIMOTHY 1:1-2

Arthur Gordon found a trunkful of one-hundred-year-old letters and got a glimpse of the value previous generations, both writers and recipients, derived from letter writing.

Most of them were written in faded ink and grimy with the dust of decades. . . . The letters were never about great historical events. They weren't passionate love letters either. They simply chronicled the lives of ordinary people: parties and picnics, business successes or failures, pets, children, the weather. They might almost have been written by my sisters to me, or vice versa, except for one thing. The emotional restraints that have become part of our daily lives were largely lacking.

The people in those generations cared about one another, enormously and intimately. And they said so, with an emphasis that was perhaps naive but was also deeply impressive. In a hundred different ways, they spoke of their love and admiration for one another, and you could feel their sincerity warm on the brittle paper. . . .

How wonderful you are! That was the steady refrain, and it made me stop and think. In each of these people, no doubt, there had been much that could have been criticized. But when you remembered the times they had lived through—the war that ended for them in poverty and bitterness and defeat, the terrifying epidemics of yellow fever—it was impossible to escape the conclusion that the writers of these letters were stronger than we are—that they faced greater tests with greater fortitude. And where did they get that strength? The answer lay in my dusty hands.[1]

A letter can bring strength and courage to others simply through its words of love. I have created a journal just for special notes and cards from friends. When someone sends me a letter I want to keep, I staple or glue it in the journal. It sits on my desk and is a wonderful source of encouragement to me. It also reminds me how little we write to each other. I have been gathering notes in this journal for many years, and it is not even close to being half full.

Twenty-five years ago, before my husband and I were married, he went away to college for a year. I have a binder full of handwritten, single-spaced letters of two, three or four pages that he wrote to me during those nine months. Times have changed. Now most of us rely on short e-mails.

When paper and ink became affordable (late 1700s), middle-class women became responsible to maintain family correspondence.[2] Many of these letters have survived. The voice ranges from the formal (as in a letter to the editor) to the informal (as in an intimate love letter). Some were written to persuade. Some were written to solidify thinking. Some were written to give strength to those struggling to overcome hardship. Some were written to express, perhaps for the first time, love and admiration. Some shaped the discourse of the nation. Some were written with no intention of ever being sent, yet they had the power to shape a soul. Letter writing is a powerful discourse.

Persuading Others

Personal letters were used to persuade others. Abigail Adams (1744-1818) was a prolific letter writer. It has taken 608 reels of microfilm to preserve the letters of her family. She wrote letters to her husband to persuade him. One of her most famous is the letter she wrote to him on March 31, 1776. It's been entitled "Remember the Ladies," and was sent as the founding fathers framed the United States Constitution.

> I long to hear that you have declared an independancy—and by the way in the new Code of Laws which I suppose it will be necessary for you to make I desire you would Remember the Ladies, and be more generous and favourable to them than your ancestors. Do not put such unlimited power into the hands of the Husbands. Remember all Men would be tyrants if they could. If perticuliar care and attention is not paid to the Laidies we are determined to foment a Rebelion, and will not hold ourselves bound by any Laws in which we have no voice, or Representation.
>
> That your Sex are Naturally Tyrannical is a truth so thoroughly established as to admit of no dispute, but such of you as wish to be happy willingly give up the harsh title of Master for the more tender and endearing one of Friend. Why then, not put it out of the power of the vicious and the Lawless to use us with cruelty and indignity with impunity. Men of Sense in all Ages abhor those customs which treat us only as the vassals of your Sex. Regard us then as Beings placed by providence under your protection and in imitation of the Supreem Being make use of that power only for our happiness.[3]

Unfortunately, "the ladies" were *not* remembered by the founding fathers. It wasn't until over a century later that woman were granted the right to vote—but Abigail's voice is preserved for future generations. Writing this letter most probably crystallized her thinking as she dreamed of the role women could play in her new country. I'm sure she and John had many lively conversations on the topic over the years.

Solidifying Thinking

Personal letters are written to solidify thinking. Sarah Moore Grimké (1792-1873) wrote letters for the purpose of building an argument, premise on premise, in order to persuade readers to her perspective. A portion of her "Letter XV: Man Equally Guilty with Woman in the Fall" exemplifies forceful, vivid letter writing. Don't assume that letter writing is passive or gentle. This letter was written by Sarah to her sister.

It is said that "modern Jewish women light a lamp every Friday evening, half an hour before sunset, which is the beginning of their Sabbath, in remembrance of their original mother, who first extinguished the lamp of righteousness,—to remind them of their obligation to rekindle it." I am one of those who always admit, to its fullest extent, the popular charge, that woman brought sin into the world. I accept it as a powerful reason, why woman is bound to labor with double diligence, for the regeneration of that world she has been instrumental in ruining.

But, although I do not repel the imputation, I shall notice some passages in the sacred Scriptures, where this transaction is mentioned, which prove, I think, the identity and equality of man and woman, and that there is no difference in their guilt in the view of that God who searcheth the heart and trieth the reins of the children of men. In Is. 43:27, we find the following passage—"Thy first father hath sinned, and thy teachers have transgressed against me"—which is synonymous with Rom. 5:12. "Wherefore, as by ONE MAN sin entered into the world, and death by sin, &c." Here man

and woman are included under one term, and no distinction is made in
their criminality. The circumstances of the fall are again referred to in 2 Cor.
11:3—"But I fear lest, by any means, as the serpent beguiled Eve through his
subtility, so your mind should be beguiled from the simplicity that is in
Christ." Again, 1ˢᵗ Tim. 2:14—"Adam was not deceived; but the woman
being deceived, was in the transgression." Now whether the fact, that Eve
was beguiled and deceived, is a proof that her crime was of deeper dye than
Adam's, who was not deceived, but was fully aware of the consequences of
sharing in her transgression, I shall leave the candid reader to determine.
(Uxbridge, 10ᵗʰ Mo. 20ᵗʰ, 1837)[4]

Letter writing has the potential to be a powerful genre in our personal development. It was through writing letters like this, back and forth, that Sarah and Angelina Grimké defined their religious beliefs and political positions. Although their father was a prominent slaveholder, both women grew up to devote their lives to abolition and women's rights. The strength of their convictions is seen in their letters.

Personal letters were also written in protest. The slave narratives arose out of private writing: men and women recording their struggles to discern what is right as they opposed what was legal. The letters of Frederick Douglass changed the conscience of the United States.[5] Public and private letter writing has been influential in the lives of men and women who faced insurmountable hardships and maintained their faith in God.

Affirming Children

Personal letters of affirmation have brought sons and daughters to faith. At a business dinner, a young woman across the table began to tell me how she had just heard the most horrible news: her friend's seven-year-old son had been hit by a car and killed. As she told me how painful the event had been, the strength of her faith in the face of such tragedy shone through.

I asked how her faith had come to be so strong. She told me of a weekend retreat when she was in high school. There had been great youth speakers and dynamic worship. Then the leader began to read aloud letters written by the teens' mothers and fathers, expressing how proud they were of their children. For some young people, this was the first time they had ever heard their father say, "I love you. I couldn't be more proud." This was a powerful experience that communicated not only her parents' love but also God's love for her. Then each student was given a manila envelope with letters from brothers, sisters, aunts, teachers and friends.

My friend told me that these letters and the experience of that weekend had deepened her faith. Now, fifteen years later as she faced tragedy, she stood anchored to the hope she has in Christ. No matter how confusing life becomes, she knows one thing is certain: Jesus loves her. We should not dismiss the impact of personal letters to affirm our loved ones.

Journaling Letters

The letter is a wonderful form to use in private journals. Sometimes I write a letter to someone who has really made me mad, or to a child who is making poor choices, or to a boss or a friend who has hurt my feelings. The form of a letter helps us to focus on what we want to express to a particular person. Beginning a journal entry as a personal letter, even if we know we will never send the letter, can help us to write very specifically.

Writing a letter to Jesus to express our heart is another wonderful option for a journal entry. It sounds a little odd at first, but many of the psalms are letters to God. For example:

O LORD, *our Lord,*
   how majestic is your name in all the earth!

You have set your glory
   above the heavens.
From the lips of children and infants
   you have ordained praise. (Psalm 8:1-2)

I have a journal devoted to letters to Jesus. Each entry begins with "Dear Jesus."

Writing a letter *from* the Lord to you also brings insight, especially using the words of a Scripture passage that you think he might be speaking to you. You might model it on the letters in Revelation 2—3. A personal letter can be very intimate and thus very powerful. Be sure to include your name in the greeting: "Dear Luann." And be sure to sign it "Jesus" or "The Almighty." I've been surprised at how writing a letter from Jesus prompts me to think about very important issues. We can very casually say, "The Lord told me . . ." but writing it down and signing it with his name is not nearly so casual a process. I don't write a letter for my boss flippantly, much less God. Maybe this is what it means to pray in his name. Obviously these letters are not inspired, but they can be very instructive.

In summary, men and women of previous generations wrote letters in which they not only encouraged and strengthened each other but also came to understand their own lives and all that they appreciated and valued in others.

You may want to begin a journal entry as a letter bringing an injustice to the Lord, or expressing your love and admiration for someone in your family. You may want to write a letter to Jesus or write a letter to yourself in his name.

The Lord can speak to us and to others in the letters we plan to send and those we plan to keep. Maybe our great-grandchildren will one day rummage through our attic and find a trunkful of encouraging letters.

A GATHERING PLACE
Keeping a Writer's Notebook

*Many have undertaken to draw up an account of the things
that have been fulfilled among us. . . .
It seemed good also to me to write an orderly account.*
LUKE 1:1-3

*Jesus did many other things as well. If every one of them
were written down, I suppose that even the whole world would not
have room for the books that would be written.*
JOHN 21:25

Reflective writing has many private benefits for the journal keeper. But there will be times when we discover something so meaningful that we'll want to take the insight out of the seclusion of private writing and revise it for public viewing. Maybe we will be asked to write an article for our church newsletter or a magazine. Our private writing contains a wealth of wisdom from all of our pondering and searching. Once it is fashioned for a wider audience and we've chosen the best form (a letter, a reflective article, a poem, a prayer) to accomplish our purpose (to entertain, edify, inform, persuade, encourage), it can be wonderfully helpful to others.

Solomon expresses the struggle of all writers to select just the right words, just the right approach to impart knowledge that will motivate people to action:

Not only was the Teacher wise, but also he imparted knowledge to the people. He pondered and searched out and set in order many proverbs. The Teacher searched to find just the right words, and what he wrote was upright and true.

The words of the wise are like goads, their collected sayings like firmly embedded nails. (Ecclesiastes 12:9-11)

We all hope that the words we write for others will be like firmly embedded nails.

A few years ago I was wrestling in my journal to understand how I could be attuned to God even when I'm busy. I knew Ephesians 5:15-16: "Be careful how you walk . . . making the most of your time, because the days are evil" (KJV). "Making the most of your time" to me always meant wisely trying to use every minute, and if you could make double use of that minute, do two tasks at once, then that was even more "godly." But all my multitasking left me feeling guilty, because I couldn't reconcile a godly life with busyness. Is it OK for a godly woman to be busy? Where is the balance?

Then, I was reading the Gospel of Mark and became very aware of how full Jesus' life was. I was set free. Jesus led a busy life! I didn't need to feel guilty because I was busy. Much of my figuring this out took place in my journal, and so when I was asked to write a news-letter article, I drew on my discoveries.

I continued wrestling with my questions, though. Then I read something Henri Nouwen wrote and I understood: Jesus could be intensely busy and yet intimately close to the Father because he was intentional about withdrawing to be with his Father. He could then take his inner sense of calm, his intimate relationship with his Father, into his busy day. I began to withdraw for longer periods of time, whole days and some overnights, just to be with the Lord. I began to learn how to take my intimacy with our Father into my busy days.

It was tremendously helpful to see that Jesus led a busy life and yet maintained an intimate walk with the Father. The issue is not how busy my life is but *how intimate my connection is*. This insight was later reshaped and expanded into a booklet I wrote.[1] And it prompted a desire to offer one-day and three-day spiritual renewal retreats for busy women. The Network of Evangelical Women in Ministry has been offering the "Oasis" and "The Springs" retreats for several years now. What I discovered and pondered in the privacy of my journal went public.

If you think you will be writing for others, then you'll want to create sections in your journal for a writer's notebook, a place where you can jot down snippets of conversation, a quote you heard, something a child said that might illustrate a point, a funny headline from a supermarket tabloid. Reading back through your entire journal after you've written the last page will help you to find illustrations from your own life as well. I also keep a page where I jot down discoveries that could be the basis for an article or a talk.

Your journal can be a rich resource to draw from when you need to write for others. You may be amazed at the wealth of insight you'll find there.

SPIRITUAL HYPOTHERMIA
When We Can't

Truly you are a God who hides himself.
ISAIAH 45:15

Though he slay me, yet I will hope in him.
JOB 13:15

Recently I went on a spiritual renewal retreat and had all afternoon to be by myself. I had looked forward with great anticipation to this time for prayer, Bible reading and journaling my reflections. But when the time came, I didn't feel like it at all. After a frustrated day I wrote:

> *I feel so blah. I feel irritable. My stomach is upset—pressure and nausea. I feel like I could punch someone. I tried writing to resolve this feeling. Nothing. I tried eating. I tried reading. I tried sitting outside. Sitting inside. Reading poetry. Taking a nap. Taking some Rolaids. Reading in bed. Nothing relieves my agitation. I'm wanting to be able to enter into the sweet intimacy of being with the Lord and enjoying his Word and prayer*

and I find myself strangely dead to all of it. In fact, I want none of it. My books don't capture my interest. Poetry didn't. Not even the book that I've been anxious to read. A whole day for me to enjoy doing whatever I want to further develop my love for Jesus and I can't.

Do you ever have days like this? Times when spiritual things are uninviting? My receptivity to the Lord is very fragile. I'm really sensitive to how I feel physically and emotionally. If I don't feel well or am emotionally upset, settling in with the Lord is a conscious choice that goes against my feelings. And there are days like this day when I simply can't.

There are also times when we feel spiritually dead. During these times we don't sense God's presence at all. We couldn't care less about him or spiritual things. Our hearts are encased in granite and nothing breaks through. We may feel cold, confused, even condemned. We may even feel like he is against us. Psalm 88 captures this:

> *You have put me in the lowest pit,*
> *in the darkest depths.*
> *Your wrath lies heavily upon me;*
> *you have overwhelmed me with all your waves.*
> *You have taken from me my closest friends*
> *and have made me repulsive to them.*
> *I am confined and cannot escape. (vv. 6-8)*

Why do we go through these times? There are several possible reasons.

Hiding Sin

The Scripture teaches that if we hide sin in our heart, the Lord will hide his face from us. He turns a deaf ear to our prayers (Isaiah 58:1-4).

When Israel was in rebellion against God, the people's love for him died. All that was left was the appearance of religion. What had been love became obligatory rule-keeping. The Holy One of Israel would not accept their offerings. In fact, he told them to bolt the doors of the sanctuary (Isaiah 1:13-15). God is not so pathetic that he needs our left-over, begrudged, fake love. He hides his face from us when we rebel against him or play the hypocrite.

I was raised going to church, so I had always known the peace of Christ. When I got into high school, I fell in love with the idea of being "cool" and hanging out with some popular seniors. One night after a basketball game, I was invited to a "wild and crazy" party. I had to make a decision. I decided to go, leaving behind all that I believed. Within days I was miserable. While I lived in rebellion against God, I lost the peace I had always known. I felt all alone. For-saken. Lost. I had broken fellowship with the Lord, and I desper-ately wanted to find him again. But I felt he was nowhere to be found. My sin separated me from God.

A month later, simply to get away from the weekend parties, I decided to go to winter camp with a bunch of friends from another church. That first night at Camp Assurance the youth pastor looked around the meeting room and said, "The Lord knows where you've been." His eyes found mine, and I knew he was right. My confirma-tion class had convinced me that God knew where I had been, and I was in serious trouble. *Guilty as charged.* Then the youth pastor said, "And God loves you." Oh, I knew that was true too. What wonderful news!

I repented and gave my life to Christ. Anyone who loved me as Jesus did, I reasoned, even when I was rebelling against him, deserved the devotion of my whole life. His peace flooded back into my soul.

As E. Stanley Jones told one of Gandhi's holy men, "I didn't find

God—he found me. I turned around in repentance and faith, and I
was in his arms."[1] If we find ourselves dead to the Lord and we know
we are in rebellion against him, the way back is through acknowl-
edging our sin, expressing our repentance and receiving his grace.

Busyness, Worry, Change

There are other times when I am not in rebellion, yet I have no passion and no sense of the Lord's presence in my life. I don't even feel
like writing. Sometimes I'm just simply exhausted, as Elijah was
after the confrontation on Mount Carmel (1 Kings 19:3-5). Caring
for babies has a way of zapping our spiritual vitality. Sometimes I've
been so busy I haven't had a minute to myself.

Sometimes the worries of this world and the deceitfulness of
wealth have choked out my spiritual passion (Luke 8:1-15). Sometimes it's change. Sue Monk Kidd found, much to her surprise, that
midlife derailed her earlier passion for the Lord: "The familiar cir-
cles of my life left me with a suffocating feeling. My marriage suddenly seemed stale, unfulfilling; my religious structures, stifling.
Things that used to matter no longer did; things that had never mat-
tered were paramount. My life had curled up into a frightening
mark of a question."

Kidd believes that in these particularly dark times we are being
asked to embark on a spiritual journey, to unfold a deeper self—the
life of Christ within us. "Is it possible, I asked myself, that I'm being
summoned from some deep and holy place within? Am I being
asked to enter a new passage in the spiritual life—the journey from
false self to true self? Am I being asked to dismantle old masks and
patterns and unfold a deeper, more authentic self—the one God
created me to be?"[2]

We can feel spiritually cold when we are grieving a significant
loss. It doesn't always happen when we expect it to. Perhaps a year

after the event we find ourselves floundering for "no apparent reason."

We could be spiritually cold because our minds are under siege and we are being relentlessly bombarded with tempting thoughts. Sometimes we find no explanation for why we feel so cold and we are simply helpless to do anything about it.

Living Through the Darkness

Ole Hallesby, a Norwegian seminary professor in the early 1900s, writes that during these times of testing we may feel totally helpless. The disparity between our beliefs and our emotions can leave us feeling like hypocrites. He encourages us not give up in despair. "Your helplessness is your best prayer. . . . Prayer is for the helpless."[3] When we are cold to the Lord and helpless to do anything about it, we shouldn't believe that he has rejected us. Far from it. He is with us. In fact our reaching out to him, even our half-hearted or no-hearted glance toward heaven, is "a result of the fact that Jesus has knocked at your heart's door and told you that he desires to gain access to your needs. You think that every thing is closed to you because you cannot pray. My friend, your helplessness is the very essence of prayer."[4] It is true.

We feel most worthy coming to God when we are spiritually alive and successfully living "the victorious Christian life" (whatever that means) and seeing God's blessings each day. But helplessness is the "real secret and the impelling power of prayer."[5] We can learn to thank God for our helplessness and actually make it a treasure, a gift from him. During these times we learn how full of ourselves we are, how much we rely on our own worthiness to stand before God rather than standing solely by his mercy through the work of Christ. These times humble us, and being humbled is a true gift from God.

Are you familiar with hypothermia? It's possible for a hiker in the mountains to get wet and lose so much body heat that her body cannot warm itself. In a state of hypothermia, one's only remedy is to strip off the wet clothes and get skin to skin in a sleeping bag with someone else—allowing another body to warm one's own.

Sometimes I'm so spiritually cold that I cannot seem to warm myself. I'm responseless. Disengaged. Apathetic. Cynicism would be better than this deadness. I've got spiritual hypothermia.

This sense of spiritual deadness is very common. Sometimes it lasts only a day, but some experience it for a year or two. Some have called it the "desert of the soul," an image of how dry and barren and alone they felt. Some have called this experience "the wilderness." Others have referred to it as the "dark night of the soul," a time when everything is dark and God's presence is not felt.

I find it comforting to remember what Matthew Henry wrote: "God sometimes hideth himself, but never absences; sometimes in the dark, but never at a distance."[6] We may feel that he is gone, but he is not. He is close even when we don't sense he is there. Spiritual hypothermia is a time when we are forced to love the Lord though nothing within us responds.

If I sense that I'm cold, I read a book with the hope that the Lord will use another author to warm me up and cause me to be responsive to his Word. Often stories warm me. Or getting time away for rest, silence and solitude restores me. Sometimes I have to pray and wait.

Yet Frederick Buechner reminds us that no matter what our experience, we are to love the Lord: "To be commanded to love God at all, let alone in the wilderness, is like being commanded to be well when we are sick, to sing for joy when we are dying of thirst, to run when our legs are broken. But this is the first and greatest commandment nonetheless. Even in the wilderness—especially in the wilderness—you shall love Him."[7]

I encourage you to write your journey through the wilderness. Pour out your frustrations to God in your journal. Remind yourself that inadequacy, unworthiness and helplessness to do anything or feel anything are not keeping you from Jesus. It doesn't matter that you feel spiritually dead. He invites you to come.

Getting Up Again

Sometimes we go through one difficult time only to find it's quickly followed by another. We can emerge from a period of darkness only to get kicked off our feet again. We wonder, where is God in all of this? Has he deliberately kicked me off my feet and left me on my own to figure out how to get back up? After reading this excerpt from A *View from the Zoo*, I now think that maybe he did:

> The zoo health center was called at 9:30 a.m. and we were informed that the female Angola giraffe was giving birth. If the veterinarian and I wanted to watch we could. Neither of us had ever witnessed a giraffe birth before, so we headed quickly for the giraffe barn. We parked and walked quietly to a location where about seven of us were afforded an earthbound view of an elevated event. I sat on a bale of hay next to Jack Badl, a man considered by most of us to be the greatest animal keeper alive. He was a man of few but well-chosen words, and when I sat down, he only nodded and continued to suck the sweetness from the alfalfa stem he had pulled from the hay bale on which we sat.
>
> I noticed the calf's front hooves and head were already visible and dripping with amniotic fluids. I also noticed that the mother was standing up. "When is she going to lie down?" I said to Jack, who still hadn't said anything.
>
> "She won't," he answered.
>
> "But her hindquarters are nearly ten feet off the ground. That calf might get hurt from the fall," I said. Jack just gave me that look that told me I had probably said something that revealed my ignorance.

I *wondered why no plans were being made to procure a fireman's net to catch the baby, so I asked. "Listen, Gary," he said. "You can go try to catch the calf if you want, but remember that its mother has enough strength in her hind legs to kick your head off, which is what she'd do if you get anywhere near that calf. They've killed lions that tried to get their calves."*

I was able to sit quietly for a while and observe the calf's journey down the birth canal. Its neck and front legs were fully extended and dangling freely, ten feet above the hard ground on which it was soon to fall. It seemed unbelievable to me that in just a few minutes this newborn was going to be introduced to such trauma. Ten feet! To the hard ground?! (It had taken me twelve years to get up the nerve to jump off a high dive approximately ten feet high into clear deep water. The giraffe calf was going to top that during its first thirty minutes of visible existence.)

The moment we had anticipated was not a disappointment. The calf, a plucky male, hurled forth, falling ten feet and landing on his back. Within seconds, he rolled to an upright position with his legs tucked under his body. From this position he considered the world for the first time, shaking some of the last vestiges of birthing fluids from his eyes and ears.

The mother giraffe lowered her head long enough to take a quick look. Then she positioned herself so that she was standing directly over her calf. She waited for about a minute and then did the most unreasonable thing. She swung her pendulous leg outward and kicked her baby, so that it was sent sprawling head over heels (or hooves, in this case). I turned to Jack and exclaimed, "Why'd she do that?"

"She wants it to get up, and if it doesn't she'll do it again."

Jack was right. The violent process was repeated again and then again. The struggle to rise was momentous, and as the baby grew tired of trying, the mother would again stimulate its efforts with a hearty kick.

Finally, amidst the cheers of the animal care staff, the calf stood for the first time. Wobbly, for sure, but it stood. Then we were struck silent when she kicked it off its feet again.

Jack's face was the only face not expressing astonishment. "She wants it to

*remember how it got up," he offered. "That's why she knocked it down. In the
wild it would need to get up as soon as possible to follow the herd. The mother
needs the herd, too. Lions, hyenas, leopards, and hunting dogs all would
enjoy young giraffes. They'd get it, too, if the mother didn't teach her baby to
quickly get up and get with it."[8]*

Remembering how we got up after we've been sent sprawling is
an important part of our spiritual growth. There is a roaring lion, a
true enemy of our soul, seeking to destroy us (1 Peter 5:8). We need
to write even during these difficult times so that we learn how it was
that we got back up.

How can we use our journals during these cold spells? Maybe, if
you sense you need to be shaken out of complacency, writing out
God's speech to Job will restore your perspective. Sometimes copying into my journal some theology on the doctrine of God reestab-
lished my faith in God's sovereignty and helped to restore my
spiritual passion over the course of several weeks.

I pray, "Lord, I believe. Help me in my unbelief," and continue to
pray it all day. I write about my doubts and expose them to truth.

I reread my journal to remind myself how God has been real in
my life.

The temptation is to abandon writing when you go through a
dark time. Don't. Record your journey. As you look back you will
sometimes be able to see why the Lord kicked you off your feet.
Hopefully you'll learn what helps you to get back on your feet.

Remembering how the Lord has worked builds a firm foundation for our faith that can help to sustain us through the long dark
night of the soul. Knowing there is a purpose in all of our darkness—our difficulties aren't wasted—can give us hope to hang on.
Sometimes it is someone else who helps to bring us back to life. Sue
Monk Kidd was helped by a monk during her dark time:

*He took his hands and placed them on my shoulders, peered straight into my
eyes and said, "I hope you'll hear what I'm about to tell you. I hope you'll
hear it all the way down to your toes. When you're waiting, you're not doing
nothing. You're doing the most important something there is. You're allowing your soul to grow up. If you can't be still and wait, you can't become what
God created you to be."*

Somehow I knew in my soul that his words were God's words.[9]

But whether we come to understand it or not, we are still commanded to love God with all our hearts. Loving him is not optional.
It's required. Let your journal help you keep your love alive. Instead
of withdrawing in silence, reach out; you may need a friend to help
warm you back up. Paul wrote to Timothy and asked him to come
before winter (see 2 Timothy 4). You too may need a friend to walk
with you. We do not know that Paul was going through a spiritually
dark time, but we do know that many close friends had deserted
him. As he faced certain death he wanted his cloak, his parchments
and his friend. There is no reason to be embarrassed that you need
the companionship of a friend, especially during times of spiritual
hypothermia. Let God use others to warm you back up. But if the
loneliness and confusion settles in like a fog all around you, as it did
for Job even when he was with his friends, continue to trust in God.

Pay close attention to your heart. Remember the hope that "the
dark night can make the difference between knowing about God
and truly knowing him. When all accoutrements of faith are
removed and we are left with the living God alone, we begin to see
him as he really is. We can never be the same when we do."[10]

30

ON A LEDGE
Risk Develops Faith

The apostles said to the Lord, "Increase our faith!"

LUKE 17:5

Have you ever stood in a deep valley and scanned the face of the surrounding cliffs, straining to distinguish a handful of climbers on the granite? I always wonder how it must feel to be one of the climbers. They say that as you scale the face of the seemingly impossible cliff, the real you comes out. In fact, they say there is nothing quite like a conversation on a two-inch ledge a mile above the valley floor to deepen a friendship, because it's when we are totally at risk that we are forced to drop all pretense and learn to trust someone else.

In a sense we are all climbing the face of a massive granite cliff. During our climb toward Christlikeness, we experience essentially easy periods when our footing is sure and the scenery incredible.

And there are other times when we are at risk, not at all sure we'll make it, when the footing is nonexistent and clouds block the sun—times when we're standing on a two-inch ledge exhausted, and we don't have the strength or the courage to continue, times when we are not even sure God is there.

This conversation about journaling is essentially a moment to catch our breath. Writing honestly can lead us out to a narrow ledge, especially if we take the risk of opening our lives to the living God. I'm convinced, however, that our journals will help us to press on, to find the faith to keep climbing in spite of the risks, discouragement and inevitable difficulties up ahead.

Taking time to journal tomorrow or the next day may begin a conversation that reveals the not-so-good side. You may feel angry or afraid—sure you'll be undone. You may feel abandoned and betrayed. You may feel as if you've taken a huge risk. You may ask yourself a hard question and end up in "the tunnel of confusion."

Like rock climbers, when we feel most at risk our faith grows as we learn to trust Jesus to lead us to safety. Jesus will meet you on the ledge no matter how afraid or at risk you feel. I pray that your journaling conversation with him will be honest, an authentic dialogue that significantly deepens your friendship and your intimacy with him.

The goal of writing reflectively in a journal, and of reading and studying Scripture, is to gain a fuller understanding of our Savior and his incomprehensible love for us. We desire to have our faith increased. This will change the way we live *from the inside out*. It is important to remember that the ideas presented here are not disciplines that somehow make us godly—at least not in the sense that if we write every day we'll earn the title. We can't think like the Pharisees, who believed that fasting twice a week made them godly men. Journaling, even journaling seven days a week, isn't the key. We seek a heart that truly believes, that is passionate for the Lord, a heart that is in love with Jesus.

For me, journaling is all about unlocking the secrets of my heart. Since the Lord loves me unconditionally, it's OK for me to take the risk of being honest about my sin and lack of faith. I am free to look at my heart's true motivation and admit where it stinks. This is very private, obviously, but essential to an authentic walk with God. In our journey toward maturity, a disciplined life of fasting, tithing, Bible study, service, prayer, silence, reflection, witnessing, solitude and journaling can be very helpful *or* it can be all wrong. Our heart's motivation makes all the difference.

Hopefully, journal keeping will not become a prescriptive, legalistic discipline that you now feel obligated to add to your devotional time. It is not prescriptive for me, so I'd hate for it to become an obligation for you. My desire is actually just the opposite. These ideas are intended to be helps, strategies, if you will, to aid us in our search for God. They are tools we can use as we feel we have the need—tools that allow us to take the risk and see who we really are, tools that help to strengthen our faith, tools that fan the flames of our devotion as we passionately pursue him. Luci Shaw rightly reminds us, "Risk demands faith and faith has eternal reward."¹

Appendix 1

FIFTY JOURNALING
POSSIBILITIES

T hroughout this book I've referred to ways of journaling that were helpful to me. This list of journaling possibilities may be a starting point as you begin to journal. You'll have a sense of what you need to write about and come up with your own journaling ideas; keep in mind that we learn the most when we seek answers to internalized problems or questions (see chapter 23 n. 2).

1. On a scale of 1-10 (10 being intimate), how close do you feel to God today? Write for a while to figure out why you are, say, an 8 rather than a 10.

2. Try paraphrasing a familiar passage of Scripture.

3. Turn a paraphrase of Scripture into a poem.

4. Copy the Lord's Prayer into your journal. As you write, expand on it.

5. The Gospel writers record Jesus asking over one hundred questions. Find some of those questions and pretend that he is asking them of you. How would you respond?

6. List all the roles that you play, your talents, your education, your exper-

tise, your friends, your ministry. Try to write several pages answering the question, *Who am* I?

7. Create a page of goals and dreams. Don't be worried about practicality, just dream. If you could go anywhere in the world, what would you want to see? If you could be anyone, who would you want to be? If you could have any job during your lifetime, what would it be?

8. What do you want to be remembered for?

9. Go back to the page(s) where you listed who you are. Now imagine that you are unable to do any of those things. Spend some time pondering the truth that Jesus' love for you would not change. If you were in an accident and had to spend the rest of your life unable to move, Jesus would love you no less than he does today. His love is not contingent on what you do. He loves you fully. Write for a while to let that truth sink deep into your soul.

10. Write about a time you felt ashamed.

11. What is "the gospel"?

12. Select a parable of Scripture and draw it with crayons or markers.

13. What ministry has God uniquely entrusted to you? What goals can you set for this ministry?

14. Consult a concordance and write out several New Testament verses that use the word *ashamed*. What does Paul say about being ashamed in 1 and 2 Timothy? Is Jesus ever ashamed? Reread what you wrote about a time when you felt ashamed.

15. Write a letter to Jesus. Begin with "Dear Jesus" and tell him anything you want. The only requirement is to be honest. Use his thoughts from the Scriptures and have him respond in letter form back to you.

16. Are you feeling squeezed into someone else's mold? Write.

17. Write out a passage of Scripture. Note your fleeting thoughts and reactions as you copy it.

18. Give yourself permission to be confused. Ask Jesus a hard question. How do you think he would answer it?

19. Write a conversational dialogue between yourself and an unsaved friend or family member. How might you open a conversation into spiritual things? How would you anticipate that he would respond?

20. Draw a picture of your spiritual journey. Write about it for twenty minutes.

21. Write a prayer for someone in your family.

22. Write down some ideas from the Scripture passage you've been studying. Write down the things that have been happening to you at work and home and church. Write down what you've been thinking about. Reflect on what the Lord might be saying to you through his Word, your circumstances and his still small voice. Can you boil this down to one sentence? One word?

23. Read Isaiah and find fifty questions God asks.

24. Brainstorm a list of the characteristics of a soldier. What does it mean to be a solider in your Christian life?

25. What are you afraid of?

26. What one thing is frustrating you the most? Why might you want it to be that way? What's in this problem for you?

27. Dialogue journal through a passage. (John 1:29-34; John 1:35-42; Luke 7:36-50; Luke 19:1-10 are great passages to begin with.)

28. Write five to ten pages of notes as you read a book. Be sure to include what you think as well as what the author thinks.

29. Write your own parable.

30. What personal risks or fears or people stand in your way of truly being able to follow hard after God?

31. What are some motivations that you may need to confess?

32. Select a topic that you'd like to learn more about, a question you'd like to answer or a problem that you'd like to resolve. Write about it. As new questions come to mind, keep pursuing the answers.

33. Find something in nature that can remind you of a character quality you would like to grow in. Take a photograph of it. Hang it on your wall. Write about it. What are the characteristics you'd like to develop? Why is this image especially meaningful for you?

34. Create a place for your devotional items; it may be a basket, or a bag, or a place at your desk. Stock it with 3x5 cards, pens, pencils, calligraphy pens, markers, special paper, watercolors.

35. Choose a favorite passage of Scripture. Make a picture using just the words of Scripture.

36. Write a letter to someone you love and send it.

37. Create a poster, not for the finished product but to enjoy the process of creating.

38. What is God speaking to you about these days? Write to discern his voice.

39. Write your testimony in a thousand words or less.

40. Whom do you admire? Choose someone you know personally. What can you learn from them?

41. Begin a list of books you'd like to read.

42. Find a secular nonfiction book on a topic of interest to you. Read it with the perspective that the author is your mentor. What can you learn from him or her?

43. Keep a travel log of your next trip.

44. Write a prayer of confession that you could use for the rest of your life.

45. What can you learn about *hearing* from the parable of the sower in Luke 8:1-15? How does the rest of chapter 8 relate to the parable?

46. Create a book of worship of your own.

47. Create your own extended metaphor of the Christian life.

48. Add an illustration to a journal entry.

49. Write a villanelle.

50. Reread the Song of Songs. Choose a favorite chapter to meditate on. Write yourself and the Lord into the story.

Appendix 2

BIBLE STUDIES

Lessons from the Desert

Read Exodus through Deuteronomy. How did God teach Moses to obey? What is the relationship between the law and God's holiness? At the rock, Moses failed to "show God to be holy." What do you think this means? Where else in the Bible is this talked about? How do we "show God to be holy"? After all Moses had been through, do you think God was unjust when he forbade Moses from going into the Promised Land?

A Life of Faith

What does it mean to live a life of faith? What does it look like? Spend some time writing your answers to these questions. Then choose a biblical character and discover what it was like for them. Both John the Baptist and Timothy are great characters to study.

The Soldier, the Athlete, the Hardworking Farmer

Spend some time reflecting on each of these metaphors from 2 Timothy 2. What are the characteristics of a soldier? the athlete? the farmer? Watch a video on war or sports or farming. Read a book to learn more. Find passages of Scripture where these metaphors are further developed. What can we learn from these comparisons? How can you bring the characteristics of the soldier, the athlete and the farmer into your life?

Appendix 3

BOOKS OF INTEREST

Devotional Reading

Abegg, Jimmy, comp. *Ragamuffin Prayers.* Eugene, Ore.: Harvest House, 2000.

Book of Common Worship: Daily Prayer. Louisville, Ky.: Westminster John Knox, 1993.

Harrison, Nick, ed. *His Victorious Indwelling: Daily Devotions for a Deeper Christian Life.* Grand Rapids, Mich.: Zondervan, 1998.

Nouwen, Henri J. M. *Mornings with Henri Nouwen.* Ann Arbor, Mich.: Servant, 1997.

————. *Seeds of Hope: A Henri Nouwen Reader.* Edited by Robert Durback. New York: Bantam, 1989.

Spurgeon, C. H. *Morning and Evening: Daily Readings.* Ross-shire, Scotland: Christian Focus, 1994 (written in 1800s).

Thomas à Kempis. *The Imitation of Christ.* 1472. Reprint, Uhrichsville, Ohio: Barbour, 1984.

Guidance for the Spiritual Journey

Casey, Michael. *Sacred Reading: The Ancient Art of Lectio Divina.* Liguori, Mo.: Liguori/Triumph, 1996.

de Sales, Francis. *Introduction to the Devout Life.* Edited by Thomas S. Kepler. Nashville: Upper Room, 1962 (written in 1600s).

Guenther, Margaret. *Holy Listening: The Art of Spiritual Direction.* Boston: Cowley, 1992.

Guyon, Madame. *Experiencing God Through Prayer.* New Kensington, Penn.: Whitaker House, 1984.

Klug, Ronald. *How to Keep a Spiritual Journal.* Minneapolis: Augsburg, 1988.

Mulholland, M. Robert, Jr. *Shaped by the Word: The Power of Scripture in Spiritual Formation.* Nashville: Upper Room, 1989.

Rhodes, Tricia McCary. *Contemplating the Cross.* Minneapolis: Bethany House, 1998.

———. *The Soul at Rest: A Journey into Contemplative Prayer.* Minneapolis: Bethany House, 1996.

Stokes, Penelope J. *Beside a Quiet Stream.* Nashville: Thomas Nelson, 1999.

Instruction in the Spiritual Life

Hallesby, Ole. *Prayer.* 1931. Reprint, Minneapolis: Augsburg, 1994.

Johnson, Luke Timothy. *Living Jesus: Learning the Heart of the Gospel.* San Francisco: HarperSanFrancisco, 1998.

Kidd, Sue Monk. *When the Heart Waits: Spiritual Direction for Life's Sacred Questions.* San Francisco: Harper & Row, 1990.

Nouwen, Henri J. M. *In the Name of Jesus.* New York: Crossroad, 1991.

———. *The Way of the Heart.* New York: Ballantine, 1981.

Shaw, Luci. *Water My Soul: Cultivating the Interior Life.* Grand Rapids, Mich.: Zondervan, 1998.

Stokes, Penelope J. *Faith, the Substance of Things Unseen: Discovering Deeper Faith and True Intimacy with God.* Wheaton, Ill.: Tyndale House, 1995.

Thompson, Marjorie J. *Soul Feast: An Invitation to the Christian Spiritual Life.* Louisville, Ky.: Westminster John Knox, 1995.

Willard, Dallas. *The Divine Conspiracy: Rediscovering Our Hidden Life in God.*

San Francisco: HarperSanFrancisco, 1998.

———. *Hearing God*. Rev. ed. Downers Grove, Ill.: InterVarsity Press, 1999.

———. *The Spirit of the Disciplines: Understanding How God Changes Lives*. San Francisco: HarperCollins, 1988.

Instruction in Reading and Writing

Adler, Mortimer J. *How to Read a Book*. New York: Simon & Schuster, 1940.

Elbow, Peter. *Writing Without Teachers*. Portsmouth, N.H.: Heinemann, 1973.

Fletcher, Ralph. *Breathing In, Breathing Out: Keeping a Writer's Notebook*. Portsmouth, N.H.: Heinemann, 1996.

Shermis, S. Samuel. *Critical Thinking: Helping Students Learn Reflectively*. Bloomington, Ind.: Educational Resource Information Center, 1992.

Zinsser, William. *Writing to Learn*. New York: Harper & Row, 1988.

Notes

Introduction

[1]Dallas Willard, *The Spirit of the Disciplines* (San Francisco: HarperCollins, 1988), p. 10.

Chapter 1: Why?

[1]Anna Quindlen, address originally prepared for commencement at Villanova University <www.top.mcttelecom.com/~tbell/Aquindlen>.

[2]*Lectio divina* is a traditional monastic art of sacred reading, of living in the gospel. Michael Casey writes, "*Lectio divina* is a technique of prayer and a guide to living. It is a means of descending to the level of the heart and of finding God" (*Sacred Reading: The Ancient Art of Lectio Divina* [Liguori, Mo.: Liguori/Triumph, 1996], p. vi). His book is very helpful in leading the way into this approach to the Scriptures and the spiritual life.

[3]Thomas à Kempis, *The Imitation of Christ* (Uhrichsville, Ohio: Barbour, 1984), 10.8.6.

[4]Linda Wagner-Martin and Cathy N. Davidson, eds., *The Oxford Book of Women's Writing in the United States* (New York: Oxford University Press, 1995), p. 4.

[5]James Britton, "The Composing Processes and the Functions of Writing," in *Children and Writing in Elementary School: Theories and Techniques*, ed. Richard L. Larson (New York: Oxford University Press, 1975).

[6]Toby Fulwiler, quoted in Tom Romano, *Clearing the Way: Working with Teenage Writers* (Portsmouth, N.H.: Heinemann, 1987), p. 19.

[7]Tom Newkirk, ed., *To Compose: Teaching Writing in the High School* (Portsmouth, N.H.: Heinemann, 1986), p. 3. See also Donald Murray, *Write to Learn* (New York:

Holt, Rinehart & Winston, 1984).
[8]Romano, *Clearing the Way*, p. 110.

Chapter 3: Steppingstones

[1]Ralph Fletcher, *Breathing In, Breathing Out: Keeping a Writer's Notebook* (Portsmouth, N.H.: Heinemann, 1996), p. 11.
[2]Peter Elbow, *Writing with Power: Techniques for Mastering the Writing Process* (New York: Oxford University Press, 1981), p. 15.

Chapter 4: J Strokes

[1]William Wilberforce, quoted in Gordon Macdonald, *Ordering Your Private World* (New York: Oliver Nelson, 1984), pp. 173-74 (emphasis in Wilberforce quote is Macdonald's).
[2]Macdonald, *Ordering*, p. 181.

Chapter 6: Pearls and Snakeskins

[1]Ralph Fletcher, *Breathing In, Breathing Out: Keeping a Writer's Notebook* (Portsmouth, N.H.: Heinemann, 1996), p. 8.
[2]Ronald Blythe, ed., *The Pleasures of Diaries: Four Centuries of Private Writing* (New York: Pantheon, 1989), p. 323.
[3]Margaret Guenther, *Holy Listening: The Art of Spiritual Direction* (Boston: Cowley, 1992), p. 13.

Chapter 7: Honesty

[1]John Steinbeck, quoted in Tom Romano, *Clearing the Way: Working with Teenage Writers* (Portsmouth, N.H.: Heinemann, 1987), pp. 41-42.
[2]Ralph Fletcher, *Breathing In, Breathing Out: Keeping a Writer's Notebook* (Portsmouth, N.H.: Heinemann, 1996), p. 88.
[3]Henri J. M. Nouwen, *The Way of the Heart* (New York: Ballantine, 1981), p. 60.

Chapter 8: Intimacy

[1]Francis de Sales, *Introduction to the Devout Life*, ed. Thomas S. Kepler (Nashville: Upper Room, 1962), p. 18.
[2]Dallas Willard, *Hearing God*, rev. ed. (Downers Grove, Ill.: InterVarsity Press, 1999), p. 214.
[3]Henri J. M. Nouwen, *The Way of the Heart* (New York: Ballantine, 1981), pp. 37-40.

Chapter 10: Three Lights

[1]Dallas Willard, *Hearing God*, rev. ed. (Downers Grove, Ill.: InterVarsity Press, 1999), p. 214.

[2]Ibid., p. 39.

[3]F. B. Meyer, in *His Victorious Indwelling*, ed. Nick Harrison (Grand Rapids, Mich.: Zondervan, 1998), p. 359.

Chapter 11: Fingerprints

[1]Abraham Lincoln, *Wisdom and Wit*, ed. Louise Bachelder (White Plains, N.Y.: Peter Pauper, 1965), p. 11.

[2]M. de Beaufort, quoted in Brother Lawrence, *The Practice of the Presence of God*, ed. Douglas V. Steere, Living Selections from the Great Devotional Classics (Nashville: Upper Room, 1950), p. 9.

[3]Louisa May Alcott, "Diary Entry at Concord, Thursday, 1843," in *The Oxford Book of Women's Writing in the United States*, ed. Linda Wagner-Martin and Cathy N. Davidson (New York: Oxford University Press, 1995), p. 501.

[4]Ibid.

[5]Elizabeth Barrett Browning, "Aurora Leigh" <www.digital.library.upenn.edu/women/barrett/aurora/aurora.html>.

Chapter 13: Go West!

[1]Anne Lamott, *Bird by Bird* (New York: Doubleday/Anchor, 1995), p. 41.

[2]Mark Wiley, Barbara Gleason and Louise Wetherbee Phelps, *Composition in Four Keys* (Mountain View, Calif.: Mayfield, 1996), p. 154.

[3]Tom Romano, *Clearing the Way: Working with Teenage Writers* (Portsmouth, N.H.: Heinemann, 1987), p. 18.

Chapter 17: A Taste of Honey

[1]Jonathan Edwards, "A Divine and Supernatural Light," in *American Literature*, ed. Emory Elliott (Englewood Cliffs, N.J.: Prentice-Hall, 1991), p. 282.

Chapter 18: In Our Own Voice

[1]George Herbert, "Psalm 1," in *The Poems of George Herbert*, ed. Helen Gardner (New York: Oxford University Press, 1961), pp. 205-6.

Chapter 19: Brushstrokes

[1]Quoted from "The Orphan Trains" <www.pbs.org/wgbh/amex/orphan/orphants.html>.

Chapter 20: Experience the Beauty

[1]Joy Sawyer's *Dancing to the Heartbeat of Redemption* (Downers Grove, Ill: InterVarsity Press, 2000) can help you grow in your reading and writing of poetry for the purpose of nurturing your soul.

[2]George Herbert, "A Wreath," in The Poems of George Herbert, ed. Helen Gardner (New York: Oxford University Press, 1961), p. 176.

[3]The sonnet is typically fourteen lines of iambic pentameter (an unstressed syllable followed by a stressed syllable—repeated five times). Often the first eight lines pose a problem, while the final six lines propose a solution. The words at the end of the line follow a rhyme scheme (there are various alternative schemes).

[4]Patricia Emerson Mitchell, "Purpose," used by permission of the poet.

[5]The villanelle consists of six stanzas. The first five stanzas have three lines each which rhyme aba. The sixth stanza has four lines and rhymes abaa. The villanelle also has a refrain—two lines that repeat throughout the poem. The first line of the first stanza is also the last line of the second and fourth stanzas. The third line of the first stanza is also the last line of the third and fifth stanzas. These two repeating lines are the last two lines of the poem.

[6]George Herbert, "The Altar," in The Poems of George Herbert, p. 21.

[7]For a full exposition of how to bring creativity and poetry into your journal see Sawyer, Dancing to the Heartbeat.

Chapter 21: Beyond Words

[1]Sue Monk Kidd, When the Heart Waits: Spiritual Direction for Life's Sacred Questions (San Francisco: Harper & Row, 1990), p. 5.

Chapter 22: Insight

[1]Henri J. M. Nouwen, Mornings with Henri J. M. Nouwen (Ann Arbor, Mich.: Servant, 1997), p. 43.

[2]Shelley Harwayne, Lasting Impressions (Portsmouth, N.H.: Heinemann, 1992), p. 3.

[3]Henri J. M. Nouwen, Bread for the Journey: A Day Book of Wisdom and Faith (San Francisco: HarperSan Francisco, 1997), Feb. 20 entry.

Chapter 23: Integration

[1]"We write to find out what we know and what we want to say. I thought of how often as a writer I had made clear to myself some subject I had previously known nothing about by just putting one sentence after another—by reasoning my way in sequential steps to its meaning. I thought of how often the act of writing even the simplest document—a letter, for instance—had clarified my half-formed ideas. Writing and thinking and learning were the same process" (William Zinsser, Writing to Learn [New York: Harper & Row, 1988], pp. viii-ix). Zinsser's book was written to show how writing is the key that opens the door to knowledge. See pages 35, 43-51.

[2]John Dewey, How We Think (Boston: D. C. Heath, 1910, rev. 1933), is often quoted as the foundational work on the difference between rote learning and reflective thought. Dewey defines reflective thought as the "active (not passive), persistent

(not spasmodic) and careful consideration (painstaking and careful, not rushed or slovenly) of any belief or supposed form of knowledge in light of the grounds that support it and the further conclusion to which it tends." Words in parentheses are from S. Samuel Shermis, *Critical Thinking: Helping Students Learn Reflectively* (Bloomington, Ind.: Educational Resource Information Center, 1992).

Shermis synthesizes a huge body of scholarly writing and distills three essential aspects of reflective inquiry: "First, *problem identification* is the heart of the process of reflective inquiry. A set of information, implications, and causes for action needs to be identified as a problem on which critical thought can chew. Second, unless students *internalize the problem* by sensing it as in some way their own, there is no reason for the rest of the process that necessarily follows. Third, although teachers may very well communicate some information to their students, critical inquiry is not primarily transmission of facts, opinions, conclusions, or plans for action" (*Critical Thinking*, p. 30).

What the body of research makes clear to me is that when we seek to increase understanding of some aspect of our life or some topic in which we are interested, we must begin with a real question or a problem that engages us, something that we are wrestling to grasp, something we desire to know. The *internalized* problem is key. As we seek to solve the problem or answer the question, we critically think our way through to a conclusion. We learn. This is critical thinking. This is reflective inquiry. This is the power of journal keeping.

[3]Zinsser, *Writing to Learn*, p. 17.

[4]Dallas Willard, *Hearing God*, rev. ed. (Downers Grove, Ill.: InterVarsity Press, 1999), p. 39.

[5]Tom Romano, *Clearing the Way: Working with Teenage Writers* (Portsmouth, N.H.: Heinemann, 1987), p. 23.

Chapter 24: Approach

[1]Mortimer Adler, *How to Read a Book* (New York: Simon & Schuster, 1940), p. 111. Adler lucidly describes the process of reading a book in order to learn. Although this book was written to help readers engage any kind of text, it is required reading in some seminaries, as its principles are insightful for how to read the Bible.

[2]Louise Rosenblatt's seminal works include *Literature as Exploration* (New York: D. Appleton-Century, 1938) and *The Reader, the Text, the Poem: The Transactional Theory of the Literary Work* (Carbondale: Southern Illinois University Press, 1978).

[3]This concept of letting truth settle from our heads to our hearts comes from Theophan the Recluse, a nineteenth century Orthodox bishop.

[4]Robert M. Mulholland Jr., *Shaped by the Word* (Nashville, Upper Room, 1985), pp. 21-22.

Chapter 25: Reflection

[1]C. S. Lewis, *The Lion, the Witch and the Wardrobe.* (New York: Collier, 1950), p. 6.

[2]For further discussion and exercises in meditation, see Tricia McCary Rhodes, *The Soul at Rest: A Journey into Contemplative Prayer* (Minneapolis: Bethany House, 1996), chap. 2, as well as her *Contemplating the Cross* (Minneapolis: Bethany House, 1998); Robert M. Mulholland Jr., *Shaped by the Word* (Nashville, Upper Room, 1985); Michael Casey, *Sacred Reading: The Ancient Art of Lectio Divina* (Liguori, Mo.: Liguori/Triumph, 1996); and Dallas Willard, *The Spirit of the Disciplines* (San Francisco: HarperCollins, 1988).

Chapter 26: Dialogue Journaling

[1]C. H. Spurgeon, *Morning and Evening: Daily Readings* (Ross-shire, Scotland: Christian Focus, 1994), April 10 reading.

Chapter 27: Attic Gold

[1]Arthur Gordon, *A Touch of Wonder* (Grand Rapids, Mich.: Revell, 1996), p. 94.

[2]Linda Wagner-Martin and Cathy N. Davidson, eds., *The Oxford Book of Women's Writing in the United States* (New York: Oxford University Press, 1995), p. 489.

[3]Abigail Adams to John Adams, March 31, 1776, in *Oxford Book of Women's Writing*, p. 491. Used with permission.

[4]Sarah Moore Grimké, "To My Dear Sister," 1837, in *Oxford Book of Women's Writing*, p. 493.

[5]"Frederick Douglass," in *American Literature*, ed. Emory Elliott (Englewood Cliffs, N.J.: Prentice-Hall, 1991), p. 493.

Chapter 28: A Gathering Place

[1]This booklet (Luann Budd, *Busyness: Our Pursuit of the American Dream*, 1997) is available for $2.00 from the Network of Evangelical Women in Ministry at <www.newim.org>.

Chapter 29: Spiritual Hypothermia

[1]Tricia McCary Rhodes, *The Soul at Rest: A Journey into Contemplative Prayer* (Minneapolis: Bethany House, 1996), p. 88.

[2]Sue Monk Kidd, *When the Heart Waits: Spiritual Direction for Life's Sacred Questions* (San Francisco: Harper & Row, 1990), p. 8.

[3]Ole Hallesby, *Prayer* (Minneapolis: Augsburg), 1994, pp. 18-21.

[4]Ibid., p. 22.

[5]Ibid., p. 23.

[6]Matthew Henry, quoted in Jill Briscoe, *Prayer That Works* (Wheaton, Ill.: Tyndale House, 2000), p. 12.

[7]Frederick Buechner, A *Room Called Remember* (San Francisco: Harper & Row, 1984), p. 41.

[8]Gary Richmond, A *View from the Zoo* (Waco, Tex.: Word, 1987), pp. 16-17. Used with permission.

[9]Kidd, *When the Heart Waits*, p. 22.

[10]Rhodes, *Soul at Rest*, p. 189.

Chapter 30: On a Ledge

[1]Luci Shaw, *Water My Soul: Cultivating the Interior Life* (Grand Rapids, Mich.: Zondervan, 1998).

Index